John Kao, who has taught at Harvard Business School, Stanford University and the MIT Media Lab, is the author of *Managing Creativity* and *The Entrepreneur*. He was trained in both psychiatry and business and has founded several companies in biotechnology, feature films, and interactive multimedia. He has also advised numerous companies worldwide. He was involved in the production of two feature films, *sex, lies and videotape* and *Mr. Baseball*. In his spare time he plays jazz piano and currently lives in Chestnut Hill, Massachusetts.

JAMMING

THE ART AND DISCIPLINE OF BUSINESS CREATIVITY

JOHN KAO

HarperCollinsBusiness

HarperCollinsBusiness
An imprint of HarperCollins*Publishers*
77–85 Fulham Palace Road,
Hammersmith, London W6 8JB

This paperback edition 1997
1 3 5 7 9 8 6 4 2

First published in Great Britain by
HarperCollinsBusiness 1996
An imprint of HarperCollins*Publishers*

ISBN 0 00 638682 2

Set in Palatino

Designed by Caitlin Daniels

Printed and bound in Great Britain by
Caledonian International Book Manufacturing Ltd, Glasgow

HD
53
K36

For Laurel, with love

ACKNOWLEDGMENTS

A book like this comes into focus through hundreds of conversations and the relationships that make them possible. Two voices stand out especially—Tony Athos, valued friend, and John McArthur, source of essential air cover. Those from whom I have learned much include Avis Bennett, Bob Carpenter, David Carson, Marni Clippinger, Jim Ferry, Brian Frankish, Shervert Frazier, Mark Friedell, Miles Gilburne, Mark Hankey, Brad Hoyt, Carol Jennings, Pitch Johnson, David Kelley, Rick Klauber, Dorothy Leonard-Barton, Ryn Martens, Gary Meller, Jane Metcalfe, Jay Ogilvy, Linda Peek, Richard Rainwater, Louis Rossetto, Paul Saffo, Hans Jörg Schwab, Klaus Schwab, Peter Schwartz, Mike Skurko, Dan Stern, Danny Stern, Tom Tierney, Jerry Welsh, Lawrence Wilkinson, and Richard Saul Wurman. Janice Pearson worked far beyond the call of duty to enable the logistics of writing. My editor, Adrian Zackheim, and Lisa Berkowitz have provided everything that an author could possibly hope for from a publisher and more.

And finally, the hands of several women shaped this effort: Donna Sammons Carpenter and her extraordinary team of creative talents at Wordworks, Inc., my agent Helen Rees for raising the notion of "full-service" to new heights, and my mother Edith Kao who got the whole thing started in the first place.

jam . . . to improvise on a musical instrument with a group: take part in a jam session (gathered after hours with their instruments and *jammed* all night)
—*Webster's Third New International Dictionary*

jam . . . to take a theme, a question, a notion, a whim, an idea, pass it around, break it up, put it together, turn it over, run it backward, fly with it as far as possible, out of sight, never retreating . . . but yes, here it comes, homing in, changed, new, the essence, like nothing ever before

—*Jamming*
The Art and Discipline of Business Creativity

CONTENTS

Introduction

THE CREATIVITY ADVANTAGE

A dozen years ago, when I said I wanted to teach a course on the art and discipline of creativity at the Harvard Business School, a distinguished colleague laughed at the idea. There was nothing new to teach about creativity, he told me, and, in any event, MBA students and corporate executives wouldn't be interested.

Well, things have changed, and no one's laughing now. The elective course I introduced in 1983 has attracted some two thousand second-year MBA students, and my executive seminars on creativity draw top executives from companies such as AT&T Corporation, Merck & Company, and Merrill Lynch & Company. Students of business and senior executives alike aren't just interested in creativity, they're fascinated by it—and with good reason. For managers, the nurture and promotion of creativity is no longer an elective. It's part of the required curriculum.

In today's new economy—nonprofit as well as for-profit—the minds of gifted people are what truly distinguish one organization from another, whether it be a software outfit, a tool-and-die shop in the renascent rust belt, an arts foundation, a messenger service in Manhattan, a town government, or a truck manufacturer in Detroit. But minds alone, however prolific with fresh ideas, are nothing without processes specifically designed to translate these fresh ideas into valued products and services.

I know: In many businesspeople's lexicon, "creativity" is right up there with "nice" in the mushy-word category. Such people had better revise their lexicons. The truth is, creativity is hard work, as almost every creative person will confirm. The great sports writer Red Smith once said, "Sure, writing is easy, you just sit down at the typewriter and open a vein." And managing creativity is, if anything, even harder work. It has nothing to do with finding a nice safe place for people to goof off. Managing creativity is much more difficult. It means finding an appropriate place for people to contend and collaborate—even if they don't particularly want to. It means scrounging from always-limited resources. It means controlling an uncontrollable, or at least unpredictable, process. Creativity, for many, is a blood sport.

Is that still too mushy for you? Consider this: Hardly a day goes by without creativity being evaluated in the toughest, most unambiguous terms we know—money. For example, when entertainment moguls Steven Spielberg, David Geffen, and Jeffrey Katzenberg formed DreamWorks SKG, they announced that they would sell a one-third stake in their brand-new company for $900 million. You don't have to be a financial wizard to infer that the founders valued their new venture at $2.7 billion, suggesting that they valued their own equity position at $1.8 billion. Not bad for a startup with rented offices, leases on the copying machines, and little if anything in the way of traditional tangible assets.

So what's the significance of the premium we put on creativity? You won't find much help under "Generally Accepted Accounting Principles," that's for sure. But creativity is valuable even so. Of course, many people do expect media and high-tech companies to assign a dollar-and-cents value to their own creativity. But wise investors should demand to know the dollar-and-cents value of creativity even in companies that sell socks, boilers, stationery, or plumbing fixtures, or deliver accounting, dog-training, logistics, or diagnostic services. After all, the success of the products or services of any enterprise depends on the creativity—or lack of it—that went into them.

Take heed of the words of people who have reason and experience to know the importance of creativity:

▶ Leon Royer, executive director, Minnesota Mining and Manufacturing Company (3M), asserts, "Either you'll learn to acquire and cultivate [creative people] or you'll be eaten alive."

▶ Southwood J. Morcott, CEO, Dana Corporation, knows that "the only way to improve your margins today is by improving your product." How to do that? "Through our ideas generation program, we expect people to have two new ideas each month. And we expect management to inplement 80% of these ideas. We believe in 'People Finding a Better Way.'"

▶ Jack Welch, CEO, General Electric Company, says, "My job is to listen to, search for, think of, and spread ideas, to expose people to good ideas and role models . . .

When self-confident people see a good idea, they love it."

▶ Marsh Fisher, cofounder, Century 21 Real Estate Corporation, says, "The real true source of power in any company today is ideas—the rest is housekeeping. . . . Ideas are the DNA of everything that is worthwhile."

▶ Bob Lutz, CEO, Chrysler Corporation, talks about the surprising success of its car model, the Neon: "For too many years, it was said that Americans can't innovate. That is changing everywhere in Detroit, and it is definitely changing at Chrysler."

▶ Marv Patterson, former director of corporate engineering, Hewlett-Packard Company, says that for HP the first step in the creativity process is "hiring the best of the best." This is how HP maintains an environment that "crackles with creativity and intellectual spirit."

▶ Michael Fradette, manufacturing consultant, Deloitte & Touche, asserts, "To make money in a disinflationary period takes real innovation and creativity at all levels of the corporation."

▶ Paul Otellini, senior vice president, Intel Corporation, believes that "Intel's history is to obsolete its old products with its next products."

▶ Lloyd Cotsen, CEO of Neutrogena Corporation, states that managing creativity is the essence of the CEO's job.

▶ Lawrence Wilkinson, president of the Global Business Network, feels that ability to improvise will be *the* key business skill of the coming decade.

I'm well aware that everything I've said begs an enormous question. Okay, you say, creativity is "in," creativity is a "must," creativity is the "way to go." But how do I get some of that good stuff for my company? For me? How do I make it happen?

In my courses I offer tough, practical answers to those questions. I show managers and future managers precisely how they can mobilize the creativity advantage by engaging their employees' minds, stimulating their imaginations, and organizing their processes, and how, by giving people the opportunity to use their talents, they can assure their loyalty. Those managerial skills pertain to every aspect of every business enterprise.

In this book, I venture—much further than I can within the boundaries of a course—to present a new vision of managers running their companies, divisions, teams, and relationships in ways that bring creativity to the forefront and multiply its benefits throughout the enterprise.

I define creativity as the entire process by which ideas are generated, developed, and transformed into value. It encompasses what people commonly mean by innovation and entrepreneurship. In our lexicon, it connotes both the art of giving birth to new ideas and the discipline of shaping and developing those ideas to the stage of realized value.

In *Jamming*, I explore the nature and sources of the creative act. It may begin with a hypothetical question like, "What if we could build tiny robots designed to scour our bodies of bacteria and arteriosclerotic plaque?" Or, "What if we could devise a guidance system that would guarantee a fast, steady flow of rush-hour traffic on major highways?" Or, "What if we could find a pesticide-cum-fertilizer with no bad side effects for the aquifer?" Or, "What if we could create an electronic community that would link the world's corporate, political, and cultural leaders in a meaningful way?" I explore how the most successful organizations have fashioned their environments to prompt such questions and help creativity flourish—how, in fact, they have transformed the traditional managerial mindset into one that welcomes and uses creativity. I also discuss how information technology—a most important new instrument in the creativity orchestra—can turbocharge collaboration throughout a company.

A future based on creativity is bright, and *Jamming* provides a guide for managers who want to be part of that future. It provides systematic procedures for taking inventory of your company's creative resources—a first step for would-be creativity managers—as well as a methodology for ongoing cultivation of those resources. The stories of creative companies show what other organizations have accomplished, not only for survival but for continued renewal. Step by step, *Jamming* helps us tap our own creativity, heighten our ability to foster creativity in others, and transform our organizations into hotbeds of creativity. To sum up, in *Jamming*, I show executives and managers that idea management must be as rigorous as the management of numbers and tangible assets.

The title of the book, which is also its guiding metaphor, I owe to my other life as a jazz pianist. When I get together with other musicians for a jam session, the group starts with a theme, plays with it, and passes it around. Suddenly the music lifts off, flies. We all fly with it. This is not formless self-indulgence or organizational anarchy. The music follows an elegant grammar, a set of conventions that guide and challenge our imagination. It is an explosion of inspiration within the art's given universe. No matter how high we fly, we always return with something new, something we've never heard before. That's jamming. The management of creativity is rich in such paradoxes. It is both an art and a discipline. Furthermore, managers must control without controlling and direct without directing, and we will see that this isn't as senseless as it sounds. Managers can't *demand* creativity any more than they can order growth from a flower.

Like jazz, creativity has its vocabulary and conventions. As in jazz, too, its paradoxes create tensions. It demands free expressiveness and disciplined self-control, solitude in a crowded room, acceptance and defiance, serendipity and direction. And, like jazz, creativity is a process, not a thing; and therefore you can observe, analyze, understand, replicate, teach, and, yes, even manage it.

Jazz starts with a whim, a possibility, a "gut feel." If the whim continues to interest us, we play with it. Our playing makes analogies and comparisons, entertains contradictions and variations. Development occurs. We get emotionally involved. Suddenly, without our even realizing it, the whim has become a distinct idea; the riff becomes a tune (in record-industry talk) or at least a potential tune. At that point, we track, measure, and guide it, refining its course.

All this is risky. Unavoidably so. When the alto sax player starts a solo, he doesn't know where he's going, let alone how far and for how long. His inner voice—to which the music, other players, the setting, and even the listeners contribute—directs him. That's the nature of improvisation, and companies that aren't willing to take its risks are not long for this fluid, protean, constantly challenging world. Companies that shun creative risks may be undercut by competitors not only with better products and services, but also with better processes and ways of perceiving new opportunities. Escaping the stagnation of the status quo, of the risk-free life, is part of the exhilaration of jamming—in music and in business.

The choice is stark. Create or fail.

1

THE AGE OF CREATIVITY

The business world is already launched on a new quest. The ancient pursuits—for capital, for raw materials, for process technology—remain eternal. But now business seeks a new advantage—delicate and dangerous, and absolutely vital—the creativity advantage.

▶ Breakfast in the Camillia Cafe in Tokyo's Hotel Okura. Coffee costs $6, an omelet $20 (and this is before the dollar's latest nosedive against the yen). I'm here to speak with a business professor named Hiro Takeuchi. When I tell him I'm writing a book about creativity, his expression turns quizzical. Not a man to blurt out his opinions, Takeuchi-san informs me in his own good time that "creativity is not a major issue in Japan." He pauses again, then adds: "No, it's the *only* issue."

▶ Now we are at the end of a long day of interviews at the Paris headquarters of Renault, where a fighting-weight company is emerging from a state-subsidized bureaucratic blimp and is en route to privatization. I ask Yves Dubriel, project director in charge of compact cars, and champion of the Twingo, Renault's snazzy new automotive child of the twist and the tango, if he has a secret for the car company's future success. "We think a lot about creativity," he answers, adding with French culinary flair, "It's a team cocktail. How we combine the mentalities—the perspectives—is everything."

▶ Here at São Paolo's Hotel Imperador, where I've just finished speaking to two hundred Brazilian executives, the reception is gratifyingly noisy. A young woman pushes through the crowd surrounding the podium to hand me a gift: A bumper sticker with her company's slogan, *"Boas ideas nacem aqui"*: Portuguese for "Beautiful ideas are created here."

▶ Red and white explosions light up the Aegean Sea's evening sky. Standing on the fantail of the good ship *Sea Goddess II*, I watch a battery of flares launched from the shore spell out a greeting to Pepsi. The senior management of PepsiCo Foods & Beverages International has gathered at this ultimate executive retreat to discuss high-performance leadership. The critical skill? Creativity.

▶ I'm at a resort hotel in Westchester County, New York, working with a team of Tiffany & Company executives. The subject of the seminar? Learning to think out of the light blue box.

▶ Today's meeting with cabinet-level representatives of Singapore's government takes place in a glass and steel tower overlooking this dynamic city-state. Its business policies have been so successful that astute visitors observe and listen carefully. What they hear is Singaporeans speaking of creativity as integral to corporate and national strategy. Today's meeting is about how to teach creativity to children. The idea is to inculcate the necessary skills in primary-school pupils by including the subject in the required curriculum. "We must start early," confides an earnest official, "if we want to keep up with the creativity race."

These are just a few stories from my own experience, but they should be enough to suggest that the business world is already launched on a new quest. The ancient pursuits—for capital, for raw materials, for process technology, for all the usual sources of competitive advantage—remain eternal. But now business seeks a new advantage—delicate and dangerous, and absolutely vital—the creativity advantage. The focus of human history has evolved from soil and rainfall and iron and coal. Now it's about the chemistry of the brain and the people whose neurons fire fastest and best. We're moving beyond preoccupation with the physical and financial to a concern for the purely human: imagination, inspiration, ingenuity, and initiative.

My obsession over the past decade has been the pursuit of the remarkably creative. I have found people and companies that know something distinctive, something too fresh to be reduced to academic principles. The expert practitioners remind me of the fabled Zen master chefs whose knives, it has been said, grow sharper as they slice ingredients. Creativity is the knife that grows sharper in the hands of the astute business practitioner.

If this is the age of creativity—and you had better believe it is—why has it come about now, in our time? And what got it going?

---

1. This is the age of creativity because that's where information technology wants us to go next.

The Nomura Institute classifies four eras of economic activity. The first three are the agricultural, the industrial, and the informational. The fourth? The creative. Just so. It is information technology that has enabled this new creative era, dramatically expanding the space for speculative thought. Information technology is evolving into the technology of relationships, facilitating the flow of creative interaction through computer-based communication networks, groupware, increasingly intelligent agents, knowledge representation and management systems, videoconferencing systems, and the convergence of different forms of traditional media.

Using their computers to access the riches of cyberspace, people tap into a host of new stimuli, challenging input, and dissonant opinions that form the raw materials of the creative process. Information technology is a medium for representing, organizing, and deploying knowledge. It can also amplify corporate awareness, allowing us to monitor our environment and to position ourselves to perceive what is genuinely new.

Everyone has a shot in cyberspace. Those new technologies qualitatively improve the basis on which people collaborate and increase everyone's potential to gain insight, share knowledge, draw from a wide range of creativity inputs, and consider and develop the widest possible array of ideas.

All companies, as Percy Barnevik, chairman of ABB Asea Brown Boveri, the $30-billion Swiss/Swedish engineering firm, observed, are information technology companies. The big difference is between those that are good at using those technologies and those that aren't.

Throughout history, commerce and manufacturing have undergone enormous change whenever information has become more widespread. The world changed radically when Gutenberg printed his first book in 1450, when Luca di Pacioli published the first double-entry bookkeeping system in 1494, and when the British Parliament passed the Public Libraries Act in 1850. The present leap has had even greater impact. Suddenly everyone everywhere has unprecedented access to information and ideas, regardless of social position or organizational rank. Everyman, Everywoman, even Everychild, can download a Library of Congress's worth of data onto a personal computer in his or her workroom or bedroom and create new value from it—for mere information is more a commodity than ever before.

Information technology has also fundamentally altered the nature of collaboration. Groupware, software that supports collaboration, brings about a phenomenon similar to the multiplier effect in economics: Moore's Law set the stage by providing the economic foundation for the information age; the cost of computing power decreases exponentially over time. Enhanced computing muscle in turn gives rise to Metcalfe's Law, which postulates that as the number of users on a network increases, so the value of the network increases at an expotential rate. I would suggest that there is another law as well: The power of creativity rises exponentially with the diversity and divergence of those users.

In traditional companies, organizational charts map the circuitry of permissible conversations and commands. Information technology abolishes the hard-wired routes, substituting flexible networks that enable people to communicate instantly and freely. Linear sequences give way to simultaneous and iterative processes. A good idea can provoke an uninhibited cascade of reactions in a hundred expected and unexpected places. These technologies of connection, and the ease with which we can change boundaries, also streamline the processes by which people interact. Boeing is only one example of a company whose information technology, in the form of design, simulation, and prototype-testing systems, enables it to reduce labor costs by eliminating unnecessary portions of the production process.

Furthermore, information technology greatly enhances institutional memory: a retrievable account of what an organization has done—who did what, with what resources, at what cost, and with what results. Even well-managed companies can suffer from a kind of corporate amnesia that allows them to persist in error, ignorance, and missed opportunities. A product development team rushes to the patent office to file, only to discover a preexisting patent filed by another group in the same company. Business comedy? No, true story. How can they do otherwise with no "past" to learn from? Information technology can become a business's single greatest path to wisdom and inspiration—to a digital remembrance of things past.

Yet mere access to information does not automatically bestow power, as it sometimes did when corporations employed intricate control systems to supply, ration, or deny such access. The crucial variable in the process of turning knowledge into value is creativity. Always more important than the tool itself is the use to which the hand directs it.

Intelligence, F. Scott Fitzgerald remarked, is the ability to hold two contradictory ideas in your head at the same time. Creativity can certainly come of such a feat: Contradiction and divergence create puzzlement, tension, and stress. And the almost instinctive desire to overcome or encompass contradiction can be achieved only with creativity. My point is that contradictions with creative potential are likely to increase on networks of information exchange. Today's creative player is someone who picks up—faster, more deftly, and more usefully than others—the conflicts that need resolution, the gaps that need filling, the hidden connections that need drawing, all the quirky, and possibly profitable, interrelationships that can be discerned in the new oceans of information. Computers generate a distinctive ease of virtual human connection at the same time that they arouse a powerful yearning for actual human connection. The creative management of those cross currents—whether in retailing or process management—will determine winners and losers.

2. This is the age of creativity because it's the age of knowledge. And in an era that prizes knowledge, creativity adds value to knowledge and makes it progressively more useful.

Companies will increasingly be measured by their knowledge rather than their physical assets. But we still must ask: What is knowledge, and why should it matter for business? Pundits speak glibly of knowledge as if it had a single definition. It's important to distinguish among different levels of knowledge. First, there is knowledge as raw material: facts, information, data. Such knowledge contains the ingredients of information clutter and overload. It's what we read in newspapers. The second type of knowledge is insight. Insight connotes *seeing into* a situation, leading to connections defined by inner perception, or representation, of knowledge: the "Aha!" Then we have ideas. Ideas are interconnected insights that we can run with. An idea is a response to the *what if*s and *if only we could*s. Finally, we have knowledge as perceived value to a customer or other stakeholder.

But it's creativity that enables the transformation of one form of knowledge to the next. For example, the nonlinear, discontinuous processing of data leads to the perception of relationships and connections, to insight. The act of perceiving relationships among insights leads us to ideas, and the creativity with which we pursue ideas engenders value. In each case, creativity comes with quantum leaps in insight and understanding that lead to value. Far from being a simple flash of mental lightning, creativity is a process with a grammar.

When we add information technology to the mix of creativity and knowledge, we get a particularly potent combination: capabilities to represent, deploy, and track knowledge coupled with technologies to promote collaboration across divergent disciplines and perspectives. When properly managed, the combination results in creative combustion.

Sweden's leading insurer, Skandia, knows this well. Since 1994, the company has systematically tracked what it calls its intellectual capital as part of its annual report and as a key to sustainable growth. It calculates leading indicators and intellectual capital ratios that allow it to benchmark its intellectual capital strategy. The company also carries out internal knowledge audits and sees them as integral to the expression of corporate creativity for competitive advantage.

Cincinnati's Senco, in the apparently low-tech business of manufacturing nails and nail guns, is another example. Senco is one of the world's most sophisticated companies in managing knowledge for creative capability. The company invests heavily in knowledge capabilities and has its own internal "corporate epistemology" or philosophy of knowledge that clearly differentiates between knowledge required for efficient operation and knowledge required for corporate advancement. Internal corporate seminars on such topics as complexity theory, and the management of imprecise systems coexist with business departments whose sole responsibility is to practice the art and discipline of corporate awareness and to bring new data, insights, and ideas to the attention of senior management.

---

3. This is the age of creativity because companies are increasingly obliged to rapidly reinvent themselves to achieve growth.

The achievement of growth via efficiency, via rightsizing, downsizing, *and* cost cutting has a limited run. And it can be a disaster for creativity, which often results from redundancy and a reasonable level of sometimes intentional *dis*organization. And to look for sources of future growth—discontinuous leaps in insight and understanding that lead to value—requires creativity. Whether it is Skandia's emphasis on renewal or Senco's concern with its management concepts, their success derives from identifying the sources of future growth—through creativity.

Bain & Company has recently completed a major study that shows that as many as 50 percent of America's larger corporations are in industries exhibiting significant turmoil. In other words, shifts in competitive dynamics—deep technological change, vanishing consumer loyalty, demographic shifts, and changes in expectations about work—are seriously unsettling those industries. Obviously, companies wishing to survive this tumult will have to find new sources of sustainable growth, even if this entails—as it surely will—reinventing their marketplace mission. Avery Dennison Corporation, a Fortune 500 company famous for its file folders and adhesive labels, is a good example of the point. The company's leaders, well aware that advances in technology will soon bring their core businesses to the edge of extinction, know they must invent—which is to say, create—new fuel, new engines, new vehicles of growth.

Corporate decision makers know that rather than simply awaiting the future, they are well advised to invent it for themselves. There is no safe harbor where companies, sheltered from the turbulence, can rethink their missions. And there are no dry docks where they can refit or rebuild their ships. In today's climate, the captains of industry have no choice but to effect change while their vessels are at sea. Moreover, you cannot simply order a make-over plan—by mail order, say, from this year's most fashionable reengineer. You forge your plans, like every other creative act, right on board. No wonder Paul Roemer, professor at the University of California at Berkeley, has recently argued that growth in the economy is related to, of all things, innovation—the development of ideas. Not the so-called productivity gains that squeeze growth from efficiency, downsizing, and rightsizing, but the ideas that drive those gains and enable companies to create the future.

---

4. This is the age of creativity because many workers today feel entitled to creative jobs, and talented people are mobile as never before.

Workers' expectations have changed substantially in recent decades. Worldwide, individuals are honing a new sense of possibility—not their village's, or their tribe's, or even humankind's, but their own. In the United States, the birthplace of individual possibility, workers have a seemingly insatiable appetite for self-fulfillment, and they crave the respect that translates into freedom from close supervision. Although their fathers and mothers could never have conceived of such "demands," today's workers insist on the opportunity to do creative work.

It's no coincidence that the era in which our younger workers grew up has been profoundly entrepreneurial—that is, individualistic. My desk runneth over with business plans from talented MBA students for whom a corner office with an impressive title just doesn't cut it. They don't want to work for big companies. They ply me for tips on how to escape corporate restrictions and tedium. MBAs are not alone in this. Many others entering today's workplace are emphatically unenthusiastic about sitting at a workstation, having to refer to an employee manual, and possibly losing their jobs when their employer decides to downsize. They are learning the new truth of employment: that everyone today is his or her own entrepreneur and that the primary qualifications for this new role are imagination, inspiration, ingenuity, and initiative—in a word, creativity. Intermediaries of every sort, from venture capitalists to talent agents, stand ready (for a price) to help those with dreams turn them into reality. More and more people, at every level, will jump the job ship to launch their own ventures unless their companies provide enough outlets for their (that word again) creativity.

If I were running a Fortune 500 company today, I would worry late into the night whether I was attracting the right kind of people, especially young people; whether my company was suffering from a "hollowing out" of talent. I would not rest until I could assure myself that creative energy, color, fascination, challenge, even exhilaration could flourish throughout the enterprise. The chairman of AES Corporation, an independent power producer with $500 million in annual sales, actually tracks his employees' job enjoyment. For a decade, he has surveyed AES employees, and the company's annual report itemizes the results: Employees consistently rank their average level of fun at eight out of a possible ten. This is neither madness nor frivolity. As we shall see, creative people run best on the high-octane fuels of play and freedom; on the pleasure that comes from being able to pose and answer the question: What if?

5. This is the age of creativity because of the new primacy of design.

Products from a wide range of industries—tools to hotels to automobiles—speak to the customer first through their design. The Black & Decker Corporation's recent redesign of many of its tools and appliances is but one demonstration of design's heightened significance. The Black & Decker hand vacuum now looks jazzier than some sports cars, and customers have greeted the new version warmly. A beautiful resort can count on an ugly brochure to turn off customers. And a grill—which in Japan is thought of as part of the car's "face"—that lacks grace can doom a new automotive model. As IBM founder Thomas Watson once remarked, "Good design is good business."

Traditionally, design is the area in which companies afford their people the greatest creative leeway. But smart companies are learning how to move beyond that. To enhance early integration of customer and corporate concerns in its new-product development, AT&T introduced its DFX framework: a design model that integrates manufacturability, environmental integrity, and ease of assembly.

In contrast to older telephones, which are inextricable amalgams of plastic, metal, and rubber, a 1994 AT&T model fits all environmental criteria for a good product. The new phone pops apart into its component, recyclable pieces. This was not just an add-on design. It exemplifies design as product essence.

Moreover, companies aren't limiting their concerns about design to their products and services; they are also addressing the designs of processes and even entire organizations. The very core of a business—its mission, goals, products, and services, as well its organizational structure and the way it pursues opportunities—are now open to consideration from a design perspective. Reengineering, the byword of just yesterday, is fundamentally about design—or rather redesign. And corporations are turning for advice on business strategy to design firms like Larry Keeley's Doblin Group in Chicago, and The Understanding Business in San Francisco for advice on how to improve access to complex information. A leader of an organization—or division, or team, or process—is its designer. In an age of creativity, after all, designing will become a larger part, even the whole, of what a leader *does*.

---

6. This is the age of creativity because there's been a change of regime in the marketplace. The customer is boss now—discerning, demanding, and no more loyal than he or she has to be. The new boss has only one question: So what are you going to do for me tomorrow? Only creativity can give the answer.

Contemporary customers want more than just a sturdy toaster: They want a toaster that automatically toasts golden brown. They don't want merely a good phone connection: They want call blocking, call waiting, caller identification, and voice messaging. They don't want an "old-fashioned" credit card: They want a long-distance phone card, an ATM card, and a debit card all in one. Customers want products—wonderful and dazzling—that they've never even imagined, and they want them now. What makes the Boss of All Bosses smile? Not the basic quality of your product or service. The consumer assumes quality, at first glance anyway. No, the clincher is as yet nameless. It's part novelty, part cleverness, part aesthetics. The creativity factor? It's the pizzazz. It's the gotta-have-it factor.

That's why, in a recent survey, many executives ranked inventiveness at the top of their list of corporate priorities. Successful corporations now concentrate on leveraging their creative capital, taking advantage of the world's exploding knowledge and of the ability of their people to mine that knowledge for clues to innovative products and services. Consider a shrink-wrapped cardboard box that contains a booklet and a set of floppy disks labeled Lotus Notes. Although to the uninitiated it doesn't look like much, and, in fact, the materials cost Lotus only a few dollars, because Lotus leverages knowledge and creativity sky high, the product went on the market at an initial retail price of $495.

Farsighted companies are developing explicit systems for representing and managing corporate knowledge. Skandia measures the value of more than thirty intellectual-capital items—its inventions—and watches over that "codified knowledge" as carefully as it guards its patents and documented procedures. In 1994, because of the critical value it assigns to its intellectual and creative assets, Skandia hired its first intellectual-capital controller. Leif Edvinsson, director of intellectual capital, understands his customers' wants and needs. Skandia, he explains, will continue its ongoing search for "wealth creators for the future."

As the crucial action shifts from physical plants to wherever talented minds collaborate, a company's relationship with its creative people becomes its most indispensable "holding." And by relationship, we can mean employment, partnership, alliance, or friendship. Today a company may outsource so many of its processes and relationships that it becomes a "virtual" organization: One that does nothing but the creative work needed to keep reinventing itself.

---

7. This is the age of creativity because the subtext of global competition is increasingly about a nation's ability to mobilize its ideas, talents, and creative organizations. A company that ignores the global creativity map is spurning an important set of strategic considerations.

If creativity springs from divergence, then what better source of contending ideas than the multicultural world stage? In an era of increasing interconnectedness, the opportunity to link cultures, to use cultural diversity in positive ways, enables creativity. Coca-Cola, a global, culture-straddling company, has long understood this. Sergio Zyman, head of marketing, has said that one of Coke's strengths is that "we have a lot of accents now." Coke employs a worldwide network of creative people and advertising boutiques. Zyman says, "We ask them to show us their successes and failures because we can cascade all that stuff around. What is starting to happen is a cross-fertilization of ideas where all of a sudden we find things that are running in Mexico that we can run in Japan, for example."

---

8. This is the age of creativity because management is transforming its role from controller to emancipator—of creativity. This is the new managerial mindset.

We're all familiar with the financial power of slam-dunking or siren-singing celebrities who sell products, draw audiences to movie theaters, and become leading figures in pop culture and pop politics. Creative people in business are enjoying the same power. Star Wars—the bidding kind—are a new reality of the business world.

How can companies retain the intellectual capital embodied in this new breed of freelancer? What resources, inspiration, and emotional linkage can you provide to encourage the stars to identify their own missions with those of your company? Since creativity is born of ambiguity, complexity, and improvisation, its quest requires specially tailored managerial techniques. The spark needs air, breathing room, and freedom to ignite. But let the air blow too freely, and the spark will go out. Close all the doors and windows, and you will stifle it.

The new managers know how to tend the flames of creativity. The leader's larger goal—which represents another managerial transformation from the Industrial Age—is the liberation of resources and talents to express themselves in ever more flexible and creative ways. Like combination game masters and patrons of the arts, leaders set direction, inspire, listen, facilitate, and provide.

To sum up: In business today—from top to bottom, from the center to the periphery—people are engaged in an irreversibly experimental way of work-life. We can take nothing—absolutely *nothing*—for granted as good, efficient, worthwhile, or tried-and-true. What's true is *trying* in the sense of trying a case, a tune, a bridge . . .

And right there is the distinctive signal of our time, resounding throughout the business world: "Testing one, two, three . . . testing one, two, three . . . testing one, two, three . . . "

But first we must test ourselves. In the chapter that follows, I provide an easy but trenchant diagnostic examination, as practitioners of medicine, might call it, whereby you can discover for yourself the creative resources in your company: where they are, in whom, what they are, and so on. Only when we have defined and evaluated our creative assets can we begin to discover the *how*—how to grasp and deploy creativity for success, how to jam.

RIFFS

In jazz, riffs are short, punchy musical motifs that can stand on their own. These are the riffs for Chapter 1:

▶ We're moving beyond preoccupation with the physical and financial to a concern for the purely human: imagination, inspiration, ingenuity, and initiative.

▶ Creativity is the knife that grows sharper in the hands of the astute business practitioner.

▶ If I were running a Fortune 500 company today, I would worry late into the night whether I was attracting the right kind of people, especially young people. I would not rest until I could assure myself that creative energy, color, fascination, challenge, even exhilaration could flourish throughout the enterprise.

▶ Creative people run best on the high-octane fuels of play and freedom.

▶ Like combination game masters and patrons of the arts, leaders set direction, inspire, listen, facilitate, provide.

2

A CREATIVITY AUDIT

Creativity is not like the weather: You can do something about it. And you can measure it well enough to determine its effects on sales and profits.

Most businesspeople will accept the idea that if they want to prevail in today's marketplace, they and their organizations urgently need to be more creative. Trouble is, they don't know how to proceed from that point, and because they don't, they fall back on the old knee-jerk arguments for not proceeding at all.

"Sure," they say, "it's great to be creative, but creativity is like rain: It falls, or not, according to the climate, and there's nothing anybody can do about it." That's the mild response. Some people react rudely and resentfully: "Give me a break! 'Creativity' is like Mr. Softee: sweet, soft, and pretty—especially when you get one with sprinkles. But Mr. Softee is better: at least I can measure Mr. Softee's sales."

Both of them are wrong. Creativity is not like the weather: You *can* do something about it. And you can measure it—not precisely, maybe, but well enough to determine its effects on sales and profits. Those effects, I can assure you, will be absolutely decisive.

This chapter is about how you can audit your company's creativity. Audit is a brutal but necessary word. It's the way we start learning the discipline of creativity. I've provided a patterned series of questions that you can put to your fellow managers, your employees, and yourself. The answers, when you find them, will give you an initial diagnostic overview of the creative processes that work—or don't work—in your business. Think of it as a sonogram.

We're looking for *creativity initiatives* here—their origin, frequency, and fate. A creativity initiative is any proposal for action-inciting change that earns at least one serious conversation with someone other than the originator's spouse, friend, or office mate. It's a conversation about creativity. Warning: If you have a hunch that creative initiatives are as common in your company as roses in the desert, then strike the words "action-inciting" and "serious." Let's not quibble: You need any sort of creativity initiative you can get.

And you need creativity initiatives for all business purposes. We all have a tendency to look for creativity in products and to forget about its importance in processes, practices, and perceptions. Such myopia can lead only to disaster. No business today can afford to neglect the need for continual renewal of its marketing, its recruiting, its accounting, its planning processes, and so on. Ditto for pedagogic creativity: improvement in the methods by which a company passes on old skills to new employees and teaches new skills to old employees. Even the realm of corporate values should support a certain kind of creativity. Businesses are not traditional societies that, with involuntary efficiency, disseminate their values through, as it were, everyone's mental DNA. The values that companies work by, and do business by, must be consciously and deliberately—that is, creatively or uncreatively—established.

Two more caveats before I spell out the audit itself. Both have to do with failure. You must concede up front that many initiatives that fail deserve to fail. Some people maintain that the criticisms that bring them down are themselves creative acts. They are certainly integral to the creative process. Criticism and judgment, however, aren't creative initiatives. They're always reactive, triggered only by another person's inspiration. Second, remember the old saw about failure: It's an orphan, while success has a thousand parents. The adage is often true-to-life and is, at the very least, a good working hypothesis for the investigator to take into the field. Spread credit as widely as possible, and blame failure, whenever appropriate, on systemic or cultural factors. Auditing creativity initiatives isn't a way to "take names and assign blame."

THE AUDIT

1. BARE FACTS

▶ What is the asset value of your creative capabilities (special equipment, people, architecture)?

▶ What proportion of your revenue comes from products less than one year old? Less than five years old?

▶ Assess your creative productivity. What percentage of the last few years' creativity initiatives have turned into actual products? Into actual improvements in business processes? Into useful changes or reinforcements of the company culture?

▶ Inventory, if possible, a half-dozen diverse creativity initiatives your company, your division, or your team—whichever is appropriate—has taken recently.

2. CREDIT DUE

▶ Who brought those initiatives to public awareness or discussion: an "insider" or "outsider"?

▶Who seconded them?

▶Who carried those initiatives to the next step, the next level, etc., all the way to their realization?

▶What conversations were key to this process?

3.   OCCASION

Under what circumstances did those initiatives arise?

▶Did they arise out of nowhere?

▶Were they in response to specific challenges? If so, whose?

▶Were they in response to benchmarking the competition?

▶Did they arise in response to an emergency, necessity, or other unforeseen event?

▶Were they the result of a well-considered corporate design to encourage or import such initiatives?

4.   DESIGN

If you believe that a company-wide creativity system stimulated a particular initiative, can you isolate the elements of the system that played a role?

▶Search and employ elements (recruitment, mergers, acquisitions, consultants, etc.)?

▶ Architectural elements (special work spaces, social spaces, etc.)?

▶ Cultural elements specifically descriptive and supportive of creativity?

▶ Pedagogical elements (on-site training, sabbaticals, mind-clearing exercises, etc.)?

▶ Carrots and sticks (bonuses, peer pressure, status rewards, etc.)?

▶ Technological elements (information networks, communications systems, gene-splicing tools, etc.)?

▶ Leadership elements (interventions by the CEO et al.)?

▶ Financial elements (investment in idea generation capabilities, slack money)?

5. TRACKING

▶ Map the progress of a sample of creative initiatives from idea to unofficial project to official project, thence to active source of company value.

▶ Pay particular attention to systemic barriers, checkpoints, obstacles, friction points, and so on, noting whether the course of action is appropriately flexible, or dysfunctionally sclerotic.

▶ Be alert, also, to human factors (jealousy and enthusiasm, alertness and ignorance, leadership support, etc.) that may stall or smooth the progress of the initiative.

6. BENCHMARKING

▶How much do you know about the procedures and cultures of your competitors? Of notably creative corporations?

▶How much do you know about the most creative company in your industry?

▶How do you foster company-wide awareness of new developments in your industry? Trade shows? Newsletters? Conferences? Customers? Creator networks?

▶Have you, in your investigations and research into the activities of the competition, found clues to your own sources of future competitiveness?

▶What hard-to-copy capabilities do you have in place that allow your company to create distinctively, continuously, and effectively?

7. PEOPLE

▶Do you know who the top creative talents in your business are, and what motivates them?

▶What is your track record in finding, attracting, developing, and retaining talent?

▶Specifically, how many key creative talents did you lose in the past twelve months and what are you doing to replace them?

▶Who's in charge of recruitment? Is it *just* human resources?

► Do your reinventing processes lead to a desired level of diversity and divergence of opinions, and inclusion of new voices?

► What, if anything, is lacking in your recruitment processes, and how and when do you plan to rectify those problems?

8. CREATIVE CAPITAL

► What systems are in place for taking stock of your creative capacities and performance?

► What systems are in place for generating creative ideas?

► What systems are in place to stockpile and protect such ideas?

► What systems are in place to realize such ideas?

► What systems are in place to reward such ideas?

We have talked about the creativity that comes from holding two divergent thoughts at the same time. Now we are going to move from talk to action, from the discipline of the audit to the art of jamming. Jamming—the impromptu, improvisational performance of jazz—is an expressive model for businesses ready to embrace the all-important practice of creativity.

3

JAMMING AND THE MANAGEMENT
OF CREATIVITY

*Jazz—like business—implies a series of balancing acts. It must
always be disciplined—but never driven—by formulas, agendas, sheet music. It must always be pushing outward, forward,
upward—and therefore, inevitably, against complacency.*

Jazz is the soundtrack of my life. The tunes vary, dictated by circumstance, or by my own inspiration and desire. Likewise the rhythm, the bass line, the tonal center. All are in some sense up for grabs, ready for improvisation. And I play this music, not in isolation, but with a host of other players whose contribution makes a difference: colleagues, family, friends, partners, clients, strangers. Even when I'm alone, I find myself at the center of an inner dialogue. I'm torn between the given and the to-be-got, between deference to tradition and the enactment of the new, between others' truths and my own. Above all, I feel the temptations of the known, of old conquests, as I fight to overcome the fear of the unknown, of new challenges as yet unmet.

But whether I am alone or with others, my practice of life and the conduct of my thoughts and actions are the practice and conduct of a jazz player: I proceed by improvisation, by jamming. Let me explain—no, illustrate—what I mean. Jamming, after all, is not only my life's guiding metaphor, it's also the metaphor that drives this book.

I unexpectedly came by my passion for jazz in an unusual setting. My parents decided not to risk my future in the wasteland of a New York City public high school, and instead sent me to a more rigorous institution, the Riverdale Country School. To make sure I would benefit from that change, they enrolled me as a boarder.

A group of African-American students in my dorm—Skip Wade, Jerry Williams, Addison Adams, and Calvin Hill—took me into their inner circle. Perhaps they were intrigued by my knowledge of classical music: I had been playing piano seriously since the age of four. In any event, these guys changed my life and my music. At night, after lights-out, we all gathered for a bull session, often about music. Addison Adams, smoking a large, thoroughly illegal cigar, would unlock his closet, where he kept his jewels: a large collection of jazz albums from Blue Note, Riverside, Prestige, Impulse—all the best labels. I'll never forget the night I first heard John Coltrane's gloriously sweet ladder of notes that accompanied the legendary crooner Johnny Hartman in their version of the ballad "Lush Life." My new friends, sitting in a circle, nudged one another, grimacing in mock-serious ecstasy over the beauty of it all. I was in ecstasy, too; only I hadn't learned yet that it was okay to show it.

Later, several classmates and I founded the Riverdale Country School jazz club. It was a way of getting the school's sanction, as well as hi-fi equipment, for listening to jazz. We were a bunch of prep-school bohemians, reading European literature, playing poker, smoking banana peels, and be-bopping along to the coolest, "most best" music in the world. All we needed were berets—ivy-covered, of course—to symbolize the college halls we were headed for.

Why would a nice boy like me—a first-generation American of Chinese origins, classically trained in music, ambitious, serious about his studies—fall so passionately in love with a form of music that many Americans consider marginal, if not subversive? Because it's dynamic, inspiring, beautiful, and, oddly enough, so useful. At its heart, jamming is about improvisation. When we have a great conversation, we are jamming. Dancing can be very much about jamming. So is the road that an inspired product development team walks to come up with something new that compels the customer's attention. When a company walks the tightrope between analytical rigor and inspired passion, when it leaves the sheet music behind for new horizons, it is jamming. Jazz has much to teach us about improvisation. Duke Ellington said, "If it sounds good, it is good." Yet most of us need to go further in order to understand.

In jazz—and in business—the improvisational style derives its power from the way it juxtaposes certain vital human tensions, or paradoxes. Here's a partial list of them, in no particular order:

▶ The established (tradition, powers that be, status quo) in tension with the new.

▶ The need for form in tension with the drive for openness.

▶ Critical norms and standards in tension with the need to experiment.

▶ The security of the familiar in tension with the lure of the unknown.

▶ Responsiveness (responsibility) to the group in tension with individual expressiveness.

▶ Discipline in tension with freedom.

▶ Power in tension with desire.

▶ Established theory in tension with persistent experimentation.

▶ Expertise in tension with freshness, naïveté.

Jazz music is called improvisational because it doesn't try to resolve those tensions. It is impervious to recipes, to formulas. It's satisfied (if that's the right word) to live them—to "work" or "play" them—for all they're worth. In classical music, the inspiration of composition leads to the sweat of rehearsal and then the decisive event of performance. In jazz, these three phases become indistinguishable parts of the same process. In jazz, and in business jamming, rehearsal *is* performance, performance rehearsal.

Note, though, that jazz tilts decidedly toward the right-hand side of those tensions. Still, we would-be practitioners of jamming—jazz musicians often acknowledge, usually obey, and occasionally get stuck in the imperatives of the past, of authority, of responsiveness, of the group, of the historically established, and so on. I think of that left side as the agenda, the manual, or more commonly as the *sheet music*. Sheet music, with its notes, expression markings, and instructions on tempo, is like an architect's blueprint—it tells us what to build. The job of a performer of sheet music is relatively straightforward: Play the music as the composer intended—without mistakes.

A well-managed enterprise can't survive without some sheet music. It allows the management of complexity, without which the modern symphony orchestra, for example, with more than a hundred performers, would degenerate into cacophony. Most large-scale human interactions require their specific blueprints, rituals, road maps, scripts, whatever, but they also require improvisation. It's not the jazz master's art alone. Conversation comes as close to being an experience of shared improvisation as you will find in everyday life. As Stephen Nachmanovich puts it in *Free Play*, a book about the power of improvisation, "You meet somebody new, and you create a language together. There is a commerce and feeling and information back and forth, exquisitely coordinated. When conversation works, it is, again, not a matter of meeting halfway, it is a matter of developing something new to both of us." But conversation still requires an underlying, all-but-invisible sheet music. "Don't look steadily into your interlocutor's eyes; don't interrupt without apology; don't raise your voice above acceptable levels," and so on, and so on.

Almost invariably, however, we try to break free of the sheet music—"light out," as Huck Finn would say— toward future possibility, toward individual authenticity and expressiveness, toward personal desire, toward the experimental. That impulse is what makes jazz—and, in business, what stimulates innovation, great strategic conversation, and corporate jamming.

But misapprehension of that impulse has also led to the widely held suspicion that jazz is licentious—freedom run amok. Nothing could be more absurd. Charles Mingus, a jazz composer noted for his inspired improvisations and protean rhythms, put it best: "You can't improvise on nothin', man, you gotta improvise on somethin'." Even in so-called free jazz, an innovation of the sixties and seventies, jazz musicians work within a structure. They agree on who is to play when, and on a loose conception of key or total center, and they let a stable beat determine a solo's rhythmic shape.

Even performers of the more conservative forms of jazz search experimentally for the "sweet spot." If it sounds too familiar, the music deteriorates to clichés. If it's too obscure, we perceive nothing meaningful from the chaos. Jazz—like business—implies a series of balancing acts. It must always be disciplined—but never driven—by formulas, agendas, sheet music. It must always be pushing outward, forward, upward—and therefore, inevitably, *against* complacency.

Today's global marketplace—turbulent, "spacey," and endlessly demanding of the new, the experimental, the faster, the better, and the cheaper—is not a concert-hall environment. There's no time for business managers to look for solutions in the archives of corporate sheet music. Today's highly competitive business world puts a premium on the skill of improvisation. All the world's a jazz club. This is an era, in short, that calls for the inspiration of art.

And discipline. The (creative) role of the manager is to work the central paradox, or tension, of the jam session: to locate the ever-mobile sweet spot somewhere between systems and analysis on the one hand and the free-flowing creativity of the individual on the other. So much is obvious. Jazz music and the management of business creativity are homologous: They emerge from the same sort of logic, a logic of the contemporary marketplace; what customers want, what sounds "good."

But one element crucial to both jazz and business that, perhaps, is not so obvious, is competitiveness. In jazz, one soloist stands up and plays *against* another. Jamming, indeed, is almost eerily metaphorical of the macroeconomic processes of capitalism. Both, in the famous phrase of the late Harvard economist Joseph Schumpeter, are characterized by "creative destruction."

Creative destruction—in the processes of product innovation—is an old story. Voice mail comes along and sends armies of office workers looking for other lines of work.

The Rabbit comes along and kills the Bug; New Tide comes in and old Tide goes out. Coke begets New Coke which fizzles leading us back to the "real thing" of Classic Coke. Sony brings a new product to market with weekly regularity—often destroying the marketability of one of its existing products. In 1776, at the dawn of industrial capitalism, philosopher and economist Adam Smith wrote, sadly but wisely, that it takes a lot of ruin to make the wealth of a great nation. If we haven't yet acclimated to that paradox, we'd better get out of business.

Here's what I'm driving at: The art and practice of creativity management call for facilitating creative destruction—for jamming. We need to have a way to deal with inspiration—a way to help us determine the winners, and to assure (or terminate) their subsequent "lives" in the productive system. Among these creative things, not incidentally, are the models of creative destruction that creativity managers come up with. I'm suggesting that the jam session is one such model—and the best.

Consider what happened at Minton's, a grungy club on 118th Street in Harlem, in 1940. Teddy Hill, a former bandleader, was managing Minton's at the time. The owner had recruited him to turn the place around. In confirmation of the relationship between the mystery of creativity and the alarm of ruin, Hill assembled a house band around drummer Kenny Clarke: Thelonious Monk on piano, Nick Fenton on bass, and Joe Guy on trumpet. At the same time, he organized a series of "celebrity nights," and threw in a free feed for musicians. "Very quickly," according to jazz historian James Lincoln Collier, "word got out that Minton's was the place to sit in." Big-name performers like Coleman Hawkins, Roy Eldridge, Ben Webster, Lester

Young, and Benny Goodman came to jam. Dizzy Gillespie was a regular. But the ferment really got going only after Clarke and Monk arranged for the group to take in a young saxophonist whom Clarke later remembered as "playing stuff we'd never heard before. He was into figures I thought I'd invented for drums. He was twice as fast as Lester Young and into harmony Lester hadn't touched." The young guy was Charlie Parker. His arrival gave birth to bop, or bebop, a development that creative types in other fields might call a "killer application."

That story is a model for corporate creativity managers: the roles and relationship of management and talent in the form of Hill and Clarke; the mix of stars and unknowns; the openness of the venue; and certainly the competitive element. Jazz devotee and poet Hayden Carruth made the point emphatically: "[I]t's a strange word, isn't it—'jam'? Many people, the pop writers, DJs, buffs, etc., have believed that it means something satisfying and good, like blackberry preserves on your bagel . . . but I think it means something competitive, even hostile." I myself wonder what it was like when everyone at Minton's suddenly realized that Charlie Parker was onto something that Lester Young couldn't match.

Mind you, no one at the time could anticipate bebop's fate. It might have faded within a few months. But those who believed in its power went on playing it, working changes in it, sponsoring it, cutting records with it, making money off it, promoting it, until at last it was fully assimilated in the eternally branching tree of (musical) life. That's all anybody can do with a creative idea. But it can be everything.

There's another aspect of jamming, however, that cries

out for as much emphasis as the creative-destructive element. In a jam session, unlike a classical music performance, there are no fatal mistakes. Yes, critics and expert audiences would allow Artur Rubinstein to miss a few notes while playing a Chopin scherzo. Why not? He brought so much to his concerts. By and large, however, classical music aficionados are unforgiving of players who don't get it right. In jazz, however, there are no mistakes, only notes that are unexpected within the underlying harmonic grammar. A note beyond the harmonic or rhythmic context is not intrinsically wrong. It is, on the contrary, the great challenge of jazz to introduce such notes into the flow of improvisation, to bring what is outside "inside," and thereby heighten or refresh the ongoing dynamic.

Metaphors are notoriously tricky tools of instruction. Nevertheless, the jam session—jazz in general—evokes penetrating questions for the creativity manager.

▶ *Who?* First, there's the question of whom you should include, and, by extension, whom you should exclude. Some people allege, for example, that the virtuosos at Minton's introduced a few of bebop's most difficult turns deliberately to exclude the less-than-virtuoso players. Should you include "everybody"—that is, all members of the whole enterprise, all inductees in the culture? Does creativity demand a particular group, one characterized by a particular level of skill, say, or style, or instruments—some sort of core competency?

▶ *Which one?* Second, there's the question of who is "minding the store," as piano great Dave Brubeck

once put it. As we've seen, the great continuing challenge of managing creativity (or being creative) is
handling the tension between art—the free play of
intuition, insight, inspiration—and discipline. "The
first recording [of "Take Five," his quartet's best-
known number] was a little stiff," Brubeck recalled
for an interviewer. "I didn't take a solo. I had to keep
that vamp locked in because we weren't used to
playing 5/4, although Paul [Desmond] could solo
well in it from the start. To this day, Joe [Morello]
likes me to keep the vamp going behind his solo.
Some nights on the tour I changed it, and he'd say,
'Hey, Bru, just keep that vamp simple. It gives me
more freedom to move around and get cross-
rhythms going.' And I feel the same way; somebody
has to mind the store, to give the improviser more
freedom to get out on his own." Again, the manager
has to choose the store minder: Will the manager set
the pace, or will he or she leave the responsibility up
for grabs? And how will the tension between minding the store and free play lead to meaningful conversation in notes, words, or ideas?

▶ *What?* Third, there's the question of the tune—
what's the agenda. The minder of the store might
get to call it, but not necessarily. It might be, and on
occasion should be, up to anyone and everyone.
Ditto for sub-questions of adherence to the tune, of
tempo and rhythm and such baseline issues. The
management of creativity involves assigning
responsibility for all those agendas; defining the
task, establishing milestones, and calling it quits.

▶ *What for?* Fourth, there's the question of The End—the end as closure, as product, as purpose, as result, as goal, or as all of the above. The manager, again, is responsible for both the definitions and the event. He or she has a deciding vote in calling a halt to the session, in defining and evaluating its "product" (if any), in drawing protective lines around it, and in determining its subsequent fate.

▶ *Where?* Fifth, there's the question of venue. Should the players convene in a rehearsal hall? Or are they ready for the jazz club? What kind of audience (or no audience at all) would be most conducive to bringing out their best performances? Anyone for cyberspace? The creativity manager must decide, or at least take responsibility for the decision.

All these questions need unpacking in detail, and that's just what I'll do in subsequent chapters. It's time to go backstage and examine the signature skills of jamming in the next three chapters. But one last suggestion before we leave this chapter: Whatever you do, be sure to set aside your old sheet music.

RIFFS

▶ Jazz—like business—implies a series of balancing acts. It must always be disciplined—but never driven—by formulas, agendas, sheet music. It must always be pushing outward, forward, upward—and therefore, inevitably, *against* complacency.

▶The (creative) role of the manager is to work the central paradox, or tension, of the jam session: to locate the ever-mobile "sweet spot" somewhere between systems and analysis on the one hand and the free-flowing creativity of the individual on the other.

▶The art and practice of creativity management call for facilitating creative destruction—for jamming. We need to have a way to deal with inspiration: a way to help us determine the winners, and to assure (or terminate) their subsequent "lives" in the productive system.

▶In a jam session, there are no fatal mistakes.

▶Throw away your sheet music.

4

CLEARING THE MIND

Fantasy, guided imagery—what I call focused reverie—are the
well-traveled paths to the cleared mind.

Aldrich 110 is a typical Harvard Business School class-room. The classic, five-tier amphitheater with its half-dozen blackboards and motorized projection screen imparts an atmosphere of comfort, focus, and drama. If the success of the learning experience depended entirely on educational architecture, the faculty could rest easy.

At the moment, resting easy is precisely what I've asked my students to do. Aldrich 110 is darkened. And the students have closed their eyes. The exercise is simple, play-ful. I read them a story that contains vignettes of life in the future—snatches of tunes, as it were, from private life and work life—that might very well be their own lives at some time or other. I say, "Imagine yourself five years in the future. Who are you with? Look around. Where are you? What do you see? Describe the sights, colors, tastes, smells." Smiles and sighs warm the room. Recordings of the students' brain waves might trace an alpha rhythm: a frequency of moderate voltage that characterizes relaxed, receptive wakefulness.

From experience, I know what is happening. The students are all inside a sort of performance space of their minds. They may be surprised, at first, by the vividness of the images with which they are playing, but soon they lose themselves completely in their diversion. Some see houses glowing in the last light of the day, and children whom they have yet to meet running across green lawns. Others are holding the hand of the person they love as they stroll along a white beach by emerald water. Then, at my signal, they hear another tune. Now, some see themselves in a corporate jet, soaring above the clouds, a drink in one hand, a phone in the other. A certain few may be shaking the hand of the President of the United

States, preparatory to advising him or her on international trade policy.

The exercise is relatively short. After six or seven minutes, I ask for the lights to go up, and we begin to talk, invariably with pronounced intensity. Students are excited, sobered, moved—all at once. Each such session surprises me anew with the richness of detail the students capture during those playful moments.

What's the purpose of this inner jam session? It's not necessarily to help students get better acquainted with their true selves or their aspirations. My goal is not "therapeutic." I want only to open the doors and windows of perception—to prepare my students for creative thought. It's an exercise, one of many I use, that facilitates *clearing the mind*.

I would like to call that process "getting to 'cool,'" except that, for most people these days, especially in the high-tech world, "cool" has come to signify a mundane "excellence." Jazz musicians use the word, however, to describe a state somebody once called "relaxed knowingness." Artists, mystics, moralists, athletes—all creative people—have their own sense of "cool." Rainer Maria Rilke, the early twentieth-century German poet, expressed that idea when he wrote to a friend: "Always at the commencement of work, that first innocence must be re-achieved. . . . If the angel deigns to come, it will be because you convinced him, not with tears, but with your humble resolve, to be always beginning, to be a beginner."

In his famous solo piano concerts, jazz great Keith Jarrett creates a forest of rhythms, themes, structures, harmonic sequences, and textures from scratch. He achieves thrilling concerts, it has been said, by "emptying himself of all preconceived ideas." Athletes talk about "getting into the zone"—the sensation that the game is playing you, not the other way around. In the realm of business, the best parallel is the "beginner's mind." We empty the mind to return to the beginning. As Shunryu Suzuki, the great Zen teacher, says, "In the beginner's mind, there are many possibilities. In the expert's mind there are only a few."

One way we can attain this mental precondition of creativity, this beginner's mind, is by forcing ourselves, or being forced, into a radical change of subject. Søren Kierkegaard, the nineteenth-century Danish philosopher, called it the "rotation method." He was thinking of crops; You can't grow corn indefinitely on the same field; at some point, to refresh the soil, you have to plant hay. The human who aims to cultivate his or her own creativity might do well to redirect concentration to subjects that are not burdened with anxiety—subjects with no connection to the task at hand.

Athletes clear their minds quite deliberately. Just before a race, the runner transforms his or her entire being into a sort of union suit flapping in the breeze. Or look at tennis players during the breaks between games: Very often you see them staring into space or plucking at the strings on their racquets. They are rotating the crops of their minds, reaching for some null point of awareness in which their spirits will find refreshment for the ordeal ahead. In feudal Japan, a samurai warrior might prepare himself for a duel to the death by sitting in a meditative state and gazing at a single chrysanthemum in a vase. *The Inner Game of Music* by Barry Green, a book inspired by Timothy Galway's *The Inner Game of Tennis*, suggests that would-be improvisers might take time to stare at their fingers or at the texture of their instrument, or otherwise refocus their attention, before they approach the music. Clearing the mind is also what business process reengineers have in mind when they instruct managers to take out a "fresh piece of paper."

In each and every case, spontaneous or traditional, the practice has the same purpose—to reorient the mind from the task-fixated self and its attendant doubts and fears, toward a nonthreatening, yet vivid world of relaxed bodies, chrysanthemums, racquet strings, the backs of fingers poised on a keyboard, and blank sheets of paper.

If there's an element of absurdity in these exercises (and, admittedly, there is), it's because absurdity, like wit, provides a quick, sure way to overthrow the tyranny of the given, the known, the "right" way, the status quo, the obsessional present. Zen masters and Christian contemplatives have long known this, and absurdist techniques are now staple fare in many training seminars.

In certain training seminars, participants may be asked to rename objects—to look at the ceiling and rename it "table," or to stare at a lamp and call it "doggie." The purposes of this apparently ludicrous game—well established in today's cognitive science—are to break the connection we habitually establish between the *thing* and our *words* for it and to push us into thinking in what Steven Pinker of the Massachusetts Institute of Technology calls "mentalese," the imagistic language of the creative mind. Pinker and other cognitive scientists have given serious consideration to the novelists, artists, and physical scientists who report that their most creative "inspirations" came to them not in words but in visual images. Albert Einstein once acknowledged that he, like many of the rest of us, got some of his best ideas in visual images as he showered. He related that he had arrived at some of his insights by imagining, for example, what it would be like to ride a beam of light and look back at a clock, or what would happen if he dropped a coin while standing in a plummeting elevator. "This combinatory play," Einstein wrote, "seems to be the essential feature in productive thought—before there is any connection with . . . words or other kinds of signs which can be communicated to others. . . . Conventional words or other signs have to be sought for laboriously only in a secondary state, when the . . . associative play is sufficiently established and can be reproduced at will."

A training seminar exercise that aims to break language's judgmental grip requires a group of people to imagine how they would like to organize, say, their twenty-fifth high-school reunion. Someone offers an idea, after which the next person's role is to say, "Yes, *but* . . . ," and offer another idea. Abruptly, then, the leader changes the rules: Now each successive speaker must pick up where the last left off, saying, "Yes, *and* . . . " That simple change, from the negative to the positive, changes the emotional pitch of the discussion, and we experience a marked improvement in openness and participation. At the same time, everyone witnesses language's role as both player and plaything of the mind.

Fantasy, guided imagery—what I call focused reverie— are the well-traveled paths to the cleared mind.

Recently, for example, I worked with a group of people charged with designing a new advertising program for the Hong Kong subway system. My request, that they tell me their ideas about the problem, elicits nothing much of interest. Time, I think to myself, to lead the group into an inner jam session. I tell them to think of a favorite scene from a movie and to mentally summon up and record that scene, with any thoughts or associations that occur to them. I mention that my own favorite is the jump-to-light-speed scene from *Star Wars*. This morning, I tell them, the spaceship reminds me of sitting in an airplane. That, in turn, reminds me that I flew into Hong Kong yesterday. I'm jet-lagged, I think, and although the sun is streaming through the window, for me, it's really eleven at night, and I'd prefer a midnight snack to the lunch sandwich I'm about to face. I map my free associations onto the whiteboard. I muse: What about food concessions? Anyone for dim sum?

My little demonstration does the trick. The favorite movie scenes of the group span a wide range, but one person and his riff seems to dominate. He's excited about a scene from the futuristic *Blade Runner*: A jet car flies past a skyscraper-sized video wall. As members of the group add their own details to his recollections, they also begin to make connections to the subject of the meeting: advertising in the Hong Kong subway. The climate in the room changes remarkably.

When I first walked into the meeting, I found a group of people engaged in somber, methodical work. After their "excursions," that same group was electrified: People excitedly interrupted one another, finishing one another's sentences. In a word, they were jamming.

Creativity begins with the *generation* of ideas. It is also very much at work in the selection, development, and implementation of ideas. When people start to brainstorm, some members of the group may simply spew derivative, top-of-mind stuff. There's no "get" to it, no reaching out. Often, though, by acknowledging the creativity of selection and implementation, the more generative participants in the group will recognize and acknowledge the off-the-shelf quality of their thinking, and will reach into new "territories" for something fresher and stronger.

Movie images were not essential to the success of that Hong Kong gathering, no more than future scenes of leisure and work life were essential to get my students jamming in Aldrich 110. The "tune" I called might just as easily have been memorable meals or the raising of the *Titanic* or words that begin with the letter C—anything interesting enough to bounce minds from conscious focus on the known, all-too-present reality. Concentration and focus on *the* problem, whatever it may be, usually narrow our thinking to the tried-and-true, shutting out access to vast storehouses of unconscious imagery and experience.

Shock techniques, applied with care, can also help to clear the mind. A legendary dean of the Harvard Law School used to greet an assembly of first-year students with the instruction that each new student should look at the people to the right and the left, and then ponder the sure knowledge that one of those two would not be returning for the second year. And Sergio Zyman, head of marketing at the Coca-Cola Company, opened a recent corporate training seminar by telling the assembled executives to imagine that they had just been fired. Also at Coca-Cola, chairman Roberto Goizueta is notorious for his "sacred cow" lectures, during which he relentlessly debunks one by one the cherished beliefs of the mainstream Coke culture. An accompanying video, which features the mournful moos of a large herd of cows, dramatizes his message.

Creative ideas also spring from the abrasion of divergent inputs. When I asked Ralph Osterhout, a well-known engineer and designer of electronic products who holds sixty-four U.S. utility patents, what he would recommend to managers who want to foster creativity in their organizations, he answered, "Magazines."

Magazines?

There's no better way to clear the mind, he believed, than to travel to strange parts of the world, and there is no easier or cheaper way to travel than by immersing oneself in the strange worlds to be found on newsstands these days. Magazines offer a cost-effective glimpse into the values, mindsets, and imaginations of other cultures.

So I often instruct my students and clients to go to the best-stocked magazine boutique they can find and buy themselves a "ticket" to a refreshingly—I mean, shockingly—alien clime. I would love to know what each one picks, but I never ask. My own choices have included *Soldier of Fortune* magazine, popular periodicals for professional surfers, and a publication about tattoos.

Looking outside for fresh input is crucial. It sounds paradoxical, but we need to know what we don't know. We need to contact what is authentically new for us, and recognize it as such through beginner's mind. I look at corporate awareness as a crucial and usually unrecognized business organizational function; as a means by which an enterprise can sense something genuinely new in its environment rather than simply talking with itself. This is not something that can be left to chance or random associations. It must be intentional, systematic, and sustained.

There are many approaches. *Forrest Gump* producer Steve Tisch talks about his need to be outside the 310 (Los Angeles) area code. For him, new ideas come from realms far afield from movies. Consulting giant Andersen Consulting maintains a Technology Assessment Group that is known, both for its "corporate monopoly on facial hair" and for being a bridge between Andersen's 32,000 employees on the one hand, and the world of hacker conferences and fringeware on the other. To maintain their freshness of perspective, the CEOs of some consumer products companies are known to make incognito store checks (an example of what might be called the Prince and the Pauper maneuver). And Rubbermaid CEO Wolfgang Schmitt has visited the Louvre to generate new product ideas. Some companies hire teenagers to surf the World Wide Web and bring back novel input. Others put teenagers to even more creative uses. The Global Business Network hired Amon Rappaport a few years ago as its "global teenager." Amon's job was to travel around the world and report his observations back to GBN. Meiji Seika, Japan's largest confectionery manufacturer, is in many respects a mainstream Japanese corporation, yet it has one manager with an extraordinary job description. Last year, he lived in Brussels, ate lunch, and visited grocery stores. His nickname: The Tastebuds.

The bottom line: Businesspeople need to cultivate awareness. They need to clear their collective minds in order to search for input that is genuinely new and provocative of creative insights.

Another approach that might be called the "intuition tickler" takes a different tack. Matsushita, the giant Japanese conglomerate that owns, among its vast holdings, the Panasonic brand, has a hundred-year plan to account for possible business and market transformations. What conceivable good, you may ask, could be accomplished by a hundred-year plan in an era whose essence is constant change? Very little. As an intuition tickler, however, its usefulness is incalculable. Forcing a company to envision an "official" future stimulates individual and collective creativity, and it nudges everyone's consideration of alternatives.

The Global Business Network holds sessions with corporate clients during which key managers may be asked to envision the newspaper headlines of tomorrow that describe various alternative futures or scenarios in which their companies will have to operate.

GBN makes a clear link between such scenario planning and the creative process. Napier Collyns, a senior GBN consultant, describes scenarios as vehicles for an "imaginative leap into the future." And he emphasizes the importance for scenario planning of generating a range of new ideas. This is accomplished by creating idea-friendly environments for divergent thinking and by including a range of voices; a process that we will later call sitting in.

Back in Aldrich 110, my students have cleared their minds. I sense the success of our exercise in a newly receptive atmosphere that pervades the classroom. The students can now hear the instruments that the creative mind—their minds—have to play. There's the trumpet of interest and intuition, the alto sax of longing and desire, the piercing insight of the clarinet, and the liquid dancing tones of the vibraphone. Their minds freshly cleared of preconceptions, my students can experience—in a nonthreatening, playful way—creative conflict and ambiguity, followed (maybe, maybe not) by a synthesizing harmony of one instrument, or an overall combination of instruments.

You might suppose that grown-up business students would need no introduction to the power of their minds. You'd be wrong. In our culture, almost everyone believes either in the romance of art or in the counter-romance of hard work. The romantics stress the stinginess of the Muses: They bestow their gifts of inspiration upon a select few, and upon no one else. The counter-romantics simply refute the romantics: Muses don't exist nor does inspiration, only luck and perspiration. Romantics fall into two groups, the very few who think they've "got it"—creativity, I mean—and the very many who think they don't. Counter-romantics don't want to talk about it at all.

The inner performances I direct in Aldrich 110 demonstrate to all but the most seriously inhibited of my students that both those points of view are wildly off the mark. Creativity, my students learn, is as natural a function of the mind as breathing or digestion are natural functions of the body.

Obviously, people whose souls are charged with mistrust will have difficulty clearing their inner minds. Furthermore, neither creative insight nor creative action comes risk-free. Some happy souls do seem to have an innate ability to ignore, deny, or somehow bracket the distrust, anxiety, even downright fear, that risk invariably arouses in the rest of us. Such people are extremely rare, and they are by no means especially creative. After all, risk is one of the mothers of invention, as well as its daughter, and that means that the risk-insensitive may simply lack good, urgent reasons to be creative. The rest of us must find ways to manage the threats to our security: We must prepare ourselves to take risks. Practice, as any musician or athlete or surgeon will tell you, is the best possible form of risk management. In business, however, would-be creative players can't simply run to the nearest official Creativity Park to practice their swing; we have to design environments, systems, and cultures that maximize the opportunities and occasions for creativity.

What, then, do we need to manage creativity's risks? Faith, if not in ourselves, then in a minimally benevolent universe, or, failing faith, a raw sort of courage that lets us clear our minds. As we shall see in the next chapter, good creativity management can bolster people's faith and courage. What management must do, above all, is define, establish, and provision a trustworthy environment. Indeed, it's in doing so that creativity managers can express their own creativity.

RIFFS

▶ In business, the mental precondition of creativity is beginner's mind.

▶ Concentration and focus on a problem usually narrow our thinking to the tried-and-true, shutting out access to the vast storehouse of our unconscious imagery and experience.

▶ Absurdity, like wit, provides a quick, sure way to overthrow the tyranny of the given, the known, the "right" way, the status quo, the obsessional present.

▶ One way we can attain this mental precondition of creativity, this beginner's mind, is by forcing ourselves, or being forced, into a radical change of subject.

▶ Looking outside for fresh input is crucial. It sounds paradoxical, but we need to know what we don't know.

▶ Corporate awareness is a crucial and usually unrecognized business function.

▶ Creativity is as natural a function of the mind as breathing or digestion is a natural function of the body.

▶ Businesspeople need to cultivate awareness. They need to clear their collective minds in order to search for input that is genuinely new and provocative of creative insights.

5

CLEARING A PLACE
FOR CREATIVITY

*What matters is creating an island of imagination amid a sea of
today's prosaic demands.*

When Charlie Parker, the great sax man, needed to work out new musical concepts, he would withdraw from the usual people, places, and things. As he put it, he would "go to the woodshed."

This may seem an odd phrase. The woodshed is a proverbial place of punishment, the spot where naughty country boys used to get a whipping. But if you think of the whippings as a chastening, a forced return to the condition of innocence, you will see that going to the woodshed is just another way to the beginner's mind.

It's also a special place, though: out of the way, unadorned, and quiet, too, if you can ignore the cries of the naughty boy or the saxophone. That's what I want to discuss in this chapter: how managers can design places or spaces that will facilitate creativity in their organizations. The good news is that, for this purpose, managers needn't start building woodsheds out behind the mailroom. The bad news—perplexing anyway—is that *all sorts of spaces* can foster creativity, and that the creativity manager had better not ignore any of them. The ideal is to turn your whole company into Charlie Parker's woodshed. Think of it not only as a physical place, but as a state of mind.

Let's look at a wish list of characteristics that you might ask for in such a place. Safe, casual, liberating. Not so small as to be limiting, not so big as to kill intimacy. Creature comfortable, stimulating, free of distractions and intrusions. Not too open, not too closed; sometimes schedule-bound, sometimes not. And so on.

It's a troublesome list, isn't it? For one thing, some elements are awfully vague—or, to be more constructive about it, full of judgment-call opportunities. What's "too small," or "too big"? Then, too, some elements seem almost contradictory. "Stimulating," for example, and "free of distractions and intrusions." Everyone knows that distractions can be stimulating. Certainly jazz players know that intrusions, in the person of a new player, can sometimes send a session soaring. Also "safe," which is in some ways, as we shall see, the most imperative characteristic of creativity-friendly spaces, doesn't always consort very well with another, almost equally imperative characteristic—openness.

In the past few decades, many creativity-conscious companies have experimented with spaces designed in accordance with the openness principle. I will describe two such companies out of thousands: the First Virtual Corporation, based in the San Francisco Bay area and Story Street Studios in Cambridge, Massachusetts.

Both companies happen to be in high-tech, but don't let that coincidence mislead you. The open office isn't necessarily a creature of modern times. On the contrary, the model owes its inspiration to the "open classroom" of the 1930s, to the newsrooms of all newspapers at all times, to the trading floors of financial institutions. At the turn of the century, for example, you could enter the Morgan Bank, and right there on the first floor, in the midst of all the comings and goings of this pivotal lending and deal-making institution, you could walk right up and speak to J.P., the great man himself. The open office is a *re*discovery, a leap back over the full-blown, industrial-era corporation and its obsessions with corner offices, washroom keys, reserved parking spaces, and private elevators. In that context, think of it as a culture-shock tactic to get *everybody* to think like a beginner.

Ralph Ungermann, formerly with Intel, was still the

head of Zilog, a company he had founded, when he started First Virtual Corporation in 1993. As its name suggests, First Virtual began with no office, no product, no personnel, not even a particular market target. It was Ungermann and an idea. His idea was to find a methodology for identifying and jumping on technology that was about to take off. He recalls, "I wanted to do something that I knew I could do: that was innovate, innovate, innovate, innovate. I wanted to bring something [to market] within a year—something that nobody else had, that would get everyone's attention, and then, a year later, do it all again. It was the idea of bringing something out that was really interesting, to see what the market wanted from it and then evolve it fast. That's really the idea, the evolving."

Evolving what? Ungermann first spotted a new desktop-video technology developed by Olivetti in Cambridge, England, that was aimed at the home market. However, if redirected at the business market, in the right way, it could potentially give birth to a new form of networking—years ahead of its expected arrival. At that point, he took on several partners, and, with almost everything from production to finance outsourced, leased an office. He wanted to get in and out of the Olivetti deal as fast as possible so he could move on to something else.

Inside the building, he designed his *mise-en-scène* in the image of his business philosophy. He created a working environment that was one big open room. It was, in effect, a jazz club. Ungermann set his own metal desk in the tightly packed room within a few feet of all the other metal desks, and he urged his "partners" to put aside their need for internal status symbols, like titles. Ideas, not fancy perks, were the currency.

"Initially everyone thought it would be a huge problem, coming to work in a big open room," he says. "People said it would be embarrassing to have visitors or answer the phone with everyone else in earshot. But that melted away instantly, and now I think it's looked on as one of our biggest assets. It gave us lightning fast communications. There are no secrets in an open room. Since the purpose here is the leveraging of ideas, it's impossible for me—or anyone else—not to have an instant grasp of what's going on in everybody's area. When a customer calls to say he's discovered a problem with a product, every single person in this company can be involved within a few minutes."

Ungermann maintains, somewhat jokingly, that the open, constantly jamming atmosphere of his company forces people not only to communicate but also to develop skills that lead to better communicating. "We invite polite confrontation. When you see a problem in someone's area, instead of saying, 'I'm going to have to talk to him next time I see him,' it's easy to talk to him *right now*. Of course, you may be interrupting him, but, hey, we techies all need to work on our social skills."

The important ingredient is openness—openness that echoes and facilitates dialogue. "I think the great breakthroughs come when you cross the boundaries from our daily focus to what other people are focusing on," says Ungermann. "For instance: People from a very big company came here to visit us and to look at our newest technology product. We sat there, chatting, and suddenly something one of them said made us realize there was an incredible way to use this product that we hadn't thought of before. Why? Because the people from that company looked at the world differently. They had a problem. We had a technology. And in that space we had that spark."

Ungermann compares his method to the traditional approach: Hold a meeting, decide on a product, and then have people disperse to their offices or cubicles to work on it. "Two months later when they come out to test what each has come up with, they find they've completely misunderstood each other. I've seen that happen over and over in product development. In this environment, that's almost impossible. It's really hard *not* to communicate and integrate."

What Ungermann and First Virtual Corporation teach us is that cross-pollination of ideas is critical to stimulating creativity. A new perspective can trigger a snowball of imagination and innovation. This can happen only when traditional barriers fall. How do companies bring those barriers down? Texas Utilities Company, based in Dallas, invited a group of local schoolchildren to sit in on a meeting whose focus was to figure out why their meetings were so long and unproductive. One young girl suggested that the meetings sounded more productive than they really were and came up with the idea of a buddy system that would enable half of the executives to miss each meeting. The company adopted her suggestion and started to tape the meetings so that people could listen to them at their convenience. Toshiba, a Japanese company, brought Europeans and Americans to its Asian headquarters in Tokyo to get an Occidental take on Toshiba's organization. Korean giant Samsung regularly sends executives to design firm IDEO's Palo Alto, California, offices to absorb creative culture. They maintain their own offices side by side with IDEO, yet pay for the right to affiliate with IDEO's "atmosphere." Hallmark, in Kansas City, Missouri, thinks nothing of flying its artists to museums across the country or the planet to stimulate their visual sense.

In short, creativity managers should rethink their basic concept of space: Shake it up. Break it down. Stretch it out.

Story Street Studios, a design company in trendy Harvard Square, proclaims a distinct culture, even aside from the post-grunge rock that reverberates through the office from an unseen CD player. The company is a high, airy, open space with a congregation of inflatable toys in one corner. Anyone in the mood—and many often are—for some high-tech fun can take a turn with *Virtual Valerie* and *Myst* CD-ROMs. In fact, the space, which, to put it mildly, at first appears disorganized, is a perfect reflection of its inhabitants' values and methodology. Story Street Studios has discovered that its blurring—even erasing—of the distinction between work and play has energized its young designers of buildings, cities, interactive media, and computer graphics. And for two good reasons. One, those designers believe that they do their best work when they can maximize free play. Two, the free-flowing physical space mirrors the truly creative person's pride and independence. There can't be the slightest suggestion of hierarchy in this conglomerate of CEOs, this galaxy of Me, Incs. For hierarchy implies bosses, and here, quite emphatically, everyone is a one-person company. Though they are hardly immune to the legends of their business generation—the rise of Bill Gates being the archetype *du jour*—and have no aversion to success, they are people who would have a difficult time fitting in a traditional corporation. They have created a place for themselves, an empire of their own, a place where creativity is king.

Techno-bohemia is a brand-new phenomenon. Cyberspace

turns out to be a welcoming place for artists and dreamers. In the past, the people who haunted cafes were poets and painters, but the cafe of the future (which has already arrived in cities around the world) has computer monitors and network connections built into the tables. No more Toulouse-Lautrecs doodling on napkins. Instead, you'll see techno-bohemians fiddling with e-mail and the Internet. Story Street is one big creative cafe, a cyber Deux Magots. One Story Streeter programs on a Silicon Graphics workstation by day and sleeps under his desk by night: a restless soul who travels the information highway without a physical address—*On the Road* circa 1996.

Anarchic as Story Street looks, however, a corporate structure exists beneath the youth-culture style. The organization is actually a coalition of several companies that have banded together. Although suits and ties are notably absent, don't mistake this crew for slackers: Many of them are the driven entrepreneurs who founded those original companies.

Story Street organizes its work around specific projects rather than along company lines. People define themselves by the venture they're working on, not the company they work for. Promoters of those projects, which usually involve interactive media in public places, walk into Story Street looking for a special set of skills to execute their visions. A large-volume retailer comes in search of the next generation of retail-interface devices. A chef seeks an interactive theme for his restaurant. The CEO of a famous advertising agency wants to create the office of the future. The head of a government agency has an idea for interactive kiosks patrons could use to communicate with the agency's home offices. A museum curator wants to stage an interactive exhibit on digital media. Chances are good that somewhere in the open latticework of Story Street's humming hive of entrepreneurs, each project will find the right combination of talents, ideas, and expertise.

Story Street is a radical experiment in physical structure—a one-room laboratory of creativity. You could say that such a structure is volatile, and it is; highly so. But remember: Volatile chemical reactions create exciting new compounds. The structure is open because the nature of the work is experimental. There is something about the experimental life that abhors enclosures of any kind.

The experience of Story Street Studios demonstrates quite dramatically that singular talents thrive, create, and produce in an atmosphere of openness that embraces work and play, side by side. Still, introducing such a climate presents its own challenges.

Exciting as companies like First Virtual and Story Street are, many feel that there are drawbacks to the idea of an open-space office. Chief among their reservations is the lack of privacy, of nooks and crannies where people can—in their search for inspiration—go off and safely make utter fools of themselves if they need to. For every hit, there are ten misses. To give free rein to your wildest imaginings in full view and hearing of the whole office can be scary, potentially embarrassing, even humiliating. We all know about performance anxiety. Even the most experienced jazz musicians join jam sessions the way prizefighters enter the ring. Even the most experienced actors get stage fright. A creative public performance is a high-wire act with no net: The stakes can be enormous.

The solution can be dead simple: In addition to open spaces, create hiding places, cozy woodsheds where people can go off and make fools of themselves in safety. A group of Lotus Notes programmers, needing to distance themselves from the Cambridge, Massachusetts, headquarters, spun out into a new company and rented a small farmhouse. There's a basketball hoop in the driveway, and inside, casual informality reigns. Kodak, in Rochester, New York, has a "humor room" filled with games, toys, creativity books, and Monty Python videos. Buffoonery is encouraged. Shiseido has shiatsu walking paths installed in many of its major facilities that enable people to walk and stimulate their acupressure points for greater inspiration. Canon, Inc., based in Tokyo, has meditation rooms. Such under-the-stairs places should be literal, three-dimensional areas, but the intangible space is equally important. What's needed is a sanctum for the shared values, perceptions, and goals of the people working on any given project. Group microcultures breed in those spaces, of course, and they sometimes run counter to the mainstream corporate culture. Knowing this, creative leadership may publicly define the space as something apart from business as usual, a semi-separate grazing ground for ideas whose integrity must be respected. The fashion for leanness—which a writer in the Wall Street Journal called "corporate anorexia"—inspired by reengineering makes this especially important. A reengineered organization, where bright spotlights illuminate every cog and wheel of the productive processes, may reduce the resources it assigns to creative efforts, leaving fewer safe havens for serendipitous creativity to take place. Magic often occurs in dark spaces, and sometimes the best thing a manager can do is turn the lights off.

It's relatively easy for a company like First Virtual or Story Street to be creative. They're new companies. Their missions are creative. They designed their structures with creativity in mind. How does the creativity manager in an older, more traditionally organized company apply these lessons? In a word: boldly. Fight for space, actual physical space where folks can go to jam. If you get resistance from above, keep fighting. What matters is creating an island of imagination amid a sea of today's prosaic demands.

Thus the need for "playpens." Michael Stern, formerly general counsel for General Magic, described that software-design company as having "a kind of insouciance and style to the place," where a rabbit runs up and down the corridors and "people walk around with parrots on their shoulders and stuff." Now if you make car parts you probably don't want animals darting in and out of the heavy machinery, but that doesn't mean you can't create a little nook where folks can go and brainstorm. (And don't limit yourself to designers. The man or woman on the shop floor has a lot of creative potential, too. In a safe space, you'll have a better chance to unleash that potential.)

The Body Shop's headquarters, filled with whimsical stuffed sculptures, Seurat prints, and a green pagoda, has been described as looking "a bit like Willy Wonka and the Chocolate Factory." Founder Anita Roddick actively embraces the "playground" image. Allstate, General Electric, and Bell Atlantic all use variations on storyboarding to integrate creativity into existing spaces. Bell Atlantic hangs large sheets of brown paper in hallways and conference rooms and encourages its employees to pick up a Post-it or a marker and add their comments and ideas. The whiteboard-covered walls of the common areas at Xerox PARC invite everyone's input.

Spatial design can indeed create tangible, physical environments conducive to creative work: spaces whose walls subtly establish an even more important psychic freedom. Various versions of the office of the future now exist and often look like some Jules Verne fantasy. The advertising agency Chiat/Day, at its headquarters in New York City, combines an unusual physical plant with a highly networked technology infrastructure: team and project rooms rather than private offices, a CD-ROM library, a conversation pit instead of a conference room. Steelcase and Herman Miller specialize in designing just such systems. Steelcase, for example, uses metaphors such as "neighborhoods," "harbors," and "activities," to replace traditional hierarchies, offices, and structures. Its designs embrace the notion of "executive community" and explicitly plan for creative combustion through the flexible combination of people and ideas. In all of this, what matters is setting aside a space that says loudly and clearly: Let those creative juices flow. And that space, like creativity itself, challenges assumptions and unleashes imagination.

Symbols and icons can also define space. Managers of creativity may need a device like the blinking red light that warns people off the soundstage when moviemaking is in progress. Dean LeBaron, chairman and founder of Batterymarch, a financial-services firm based in Boston, tells about one colleague who came up with a way to deal with the problems of an open office. The man brought in a hat that belonged to one of his children. The hat had a light on top that could be switched on and off. If the man was wearing the hat with the light off, he was thinking but could be disturbed; hat on and light on meant he was thinking and couldn't be disturbed; no hat on meant talk away.

A video game company called Activision established innovative boundaries for its people. In the early 1980s, the company effectively isolated its creative teams, with fewer than ten people acting as intermediaries—so-called creative design managers—from the rest of the organization. Designers communicated chiefly with one another, like Cabots talking only to Lodges. The message was that creative people are stars. A similar company, called Imagic, which initiated its operations in Los Gatos, California, did not want a creative aristocracy. Placing its game designers on integrated teams, it made heavy use of marketing input and concept testing before producing new games. Which approach was right? The proper answer is: Both. It is important to focus on both sensational ideas and the designers that create them, but also to capitalize on collaboration and diversity. To paraphrase Forrest Gump, creativity is as creativity does.

Boundaries provide safety, but safety and isolation often breed teams with the collaborative spirit of semi-secret societies—aka conspiracies. These subcultures can be disruptive to cooperation throughout the full organization. Groups identifiable by the special treatment they enjoy often become focal points for "sibling" rivalry. Resentment and jealousy among mainstream workers and managers can increase the difficulty of coordinating complex activities.

Despite this, managers should be willing to risk encouraging a subcultural identity that can support a new creative initiative. For example, when design firm IDEO was confronted by a group of young dissident designers who did not feel comfortable in IDEO's already leading-edge creative environment, they were encouraged to create their own working space and to operate under the maverick identity "Spunkworks." Trite, although often practiced, versions of this encouragement can take the form of giving the task group or team distinctive names and logos. Managers can supply team hats or signs for the members' desks, anything to encourage a brand identity for creativity. For example, Apple Computer was the site of the now-famous pirate flag that adorned its Macintosh facility in its heyday. More substantively, management can reinforce that special identity by creating an alternative infrastructure—providing networked communications, locating the group off-site, giving it access to resources and information, or offering extra perks.

The opportunities and challenges become even greater when organizations move from physical places to virtual spaces. Take VeriFone, a company that solves the openness-versus-safety dilemma by zapping it. The company is so wide open—that is, globally decentralized, with no HQ at all—that everyone is assured the safety of privacy. The world's leading merchant of "Transaction Automation Solutions," chiefly automated credit card verification systems, is about as decentralized as a global company can be. Hatim Tyabji, president and CEO since 1986, calls it a blueberry pancake. Each of the twenty-nine berry locations—in Costa Mesa, California; Madrid; Milan; Taipei; Tokyo; Beijing; Bangalore; and so on—is equally important. All the sites feed from an enormous common database. All are (virtually) next door to all others via leased telephone lines that transmit the company's Digital VAXmail, an e-mail system reinforced by heavy use of videoconferencing. VeriFone never sleeps: Operations are continuous, twenty-four hours a day, seven days a week. The company is a practitioner of digital baton passing, three shifts a day. Its motto is: "Be online or die."

And most of the employees are literally up in the air. A third of them are on a plane at any given time, at a cost of more than $5 million a year in airfare and hotel bills alone. Tyabji himself logs about four hundred thousand air miles annually, an average of fifteen hundred miles a business day. E-mail traffic can come to one hundred messages per person per day, one million per month.

The combination of physical decentralization and telecommunications unity gives the company a remarkable capacity for quick and creative response. The network is a catalyst for creativity. When a major competitor was about to launch a new marketing plan, VeriFone, which had received an early warning, took just five hours to prepare a counterattack and get its action plan to every station. When the company adopted its own new marketing program aimed at smaller retailers, discussions on the electronic network reduced implementation time to just one week.

Unrelentingly innovative, VeriFone spends 12 percent of its revenue on R&D. It had so out-invented its competition by the end of the 1980s that it began expanding into technology for supermarkets, gasoline stations, and food-stamp purchases. Now it has taken itself, and us, to the verge of the worldwide cash-automation era, when "smart cards"—with microprocessors and memory for storing value—will replace cash for many low-cost purchases. More than a million businesses outside the United States use its systems. VeriFone's combination of novel products and a decentralized global organization has captured 60 percent of the world retail market, and produced an incredible annual growth rate of 20 percent. VeriFone has its own definition of creative space. Every company—no matter what its industry—must learn from VeriFone's example in fashioning its own unique response to the need for virtual spaces as well as physical places.

First Virtual, Story Street, and VeriFone represent three distinct responses to the imperative of place, of building a "woodshed." Each organization found the right solution—the right solution for its own personality. Place is essential to creativity, and the construction, or deconstruction, of place can be every bit as creative as anything that occurs within its confines. At its heart, place confers tangibility to creativity, that most intangible of processes, and in doing so, enhances the belief in its attainability. This is a challenge that every creativity manager must address. There could very well be a Charlie Parker in your company, but without the right place or space you may never know it.

RIFFS

▶ Places or spaces that facilitate creativity in their organizations are safe, casual, liberating. Not so small as to be limiting, not so big as to kill intimacy. Creature comfortable, stimulating, free of distractions and intrusions. Not too open, not too closed; sometimes time-bound, sometimes not.

▶ The open, constantly jamming atmosphere of certain companies forces people not only to communicate but also to develop skills that lead to better communicating.

▶Creative structures are volatile, highly so. But remember: Volatile chemical reactions create exciting new compounds. The structure is open because the nature of the work is experimental.

▶A creative public performance is a high-wire act with no net: The stakes can be enormous. In addition to open spaces, create hiding places, cozy attics where people can go off and make fools of themselves in perfect safety.

▶Spatial design can create tangible, physical environments conducive to creative work: spaces whose material walls subtly establish psychic freedom.

6

CLEARING THE BELIEFS

The most important thing is to infuse, imbue, and instill a respect for and belief in the power of creativity throughout your company.

A startling sight greets first-time visitors to the cafeteria of hearing-aid maker Oticon in Hellerup, Denmark. Smack in the middle of the room, a huge transparent plastic pipe runs from floor to ceiling. During the course of the day—lightly at lunch, heavily in the morning and at quitting time—a snowfall of paper drifts down the tube.

That transparent tube is a powerful symbol. A symbol backed up by action. At Oticon only one person handles each piece of paper—to enter its useful information into a database, shred the paper, and then send it down the tube. It's a vivid reminder to everyone in the building that Oticon is striving to become a paperless office, and therefore a rapid-response business. This aversion to paper encourages people to talk to one another, bounce ideas around, mix it up. The company's physical plant is designed to facilitate this give-and-take. Headquarters is in an old Tuborg brewery (fermentation being a neat symbol for a creativity-conscious company). Connecting the floors is a spiral staircase, intentionally designed to be wide enough for people to stop and talk during chance encounters. Each floor has a coffee bar for schmoozing. Finally, at Oticon, your "office" consists of a credenza on wheels, and you can move it wherever you want to be, wherever your work takes you.

All this stagecraft is part of a deliberate effort to create a culture of creativity. To turn Oticon into a company where innovation is the norm, where everyone is encouraged to use ingenuity and imagination, and where corporate jamming happens. The company has cultivated its ability to improvise, to create a continuing internal dialogue that leads to better products and stronger profits. Oticon views a creative culture as the linchpin of its corporate strategy. Says CEO Lars Kolind, "We want to develop our creative capabilities to the point where they cannot be copied." And to do this, Kolind repeatedly stresses a core Oticon value, "Think the unthinkable," that was drawn from his initial manifesto for turning the company around and reinjecting into it a sense of creative urgency.

How can you develop these creative capabilities in your company? Jamming, whether in music or in business, is about belief. Belief gets you from zero to one. That's what this chapter is all about.

Success depends on your ability to infuse, imbue, and instill a respect for and belief in the power of creativity throughout your company. This isn't a dictum that you can deliver from on high—although that's where it starts—it must become part of a company's personality, the cornerstone of its modus operandi. It's useless and hypocritical to spout a lot of talk about creativity and then retain processes that deaden imagination and spirit. You must show people—in concrete ways—that your company values their ingenuity, their inventiveness, their spark, and their soul.

Sound like a tall order? Yes and no. Expectations, standards, and style have to change if you're going to create a culture that truly values creativity: It's a painful process that demands commitment, but once changes start to register, a snowball effect kicks in: Creativity begets spontaneity begets stimulation begets invention—you get the idea. The end result? A company—no matter what its industry—that's bold, innovative, imaginative, and profitable.

The first step in making your company a happening place is to kick out the crutches that support a creativity-deadening culture. A reliance on obfuscating paper is one such crutch. All those plans, reports, charts, systems, and procedures could knock the wind out of any jazz musician's lungs. Throw away the sheet music. Start creative conversations.

When Kolind joined Oticon in 1987, the proud old company was wedded to paper: It was a house of cards where everything was written down—and had been for ninety years. Kolind ignored the constricting old sheet music and trumpeted the advent of corporate jamming. He dissolved the entire formal organization, did away with titles and job descriptions, abolished specialization. He instituted instead the notion of the multi-job, the idea being that everyone should be responsible for doing not only what they were trained to do but what interests them beyond their specialty. Shortly after his arrival, he was asked to kill a proposed new behind-the-ear hearing aid. Although the new model's automatic adjustment to sound levels freed the user from fiddling with the volume control, just about everyone at Oticon insisted it was a loser. Hey, they had it in writing: People wanted a small in-the-ear device. Kolind shredded the paper and ordered his designers to come up with a snazzy, high-tech model. It didn't take long for Oticon's new product to grab a hefty share of the hearing-aid market. Since then, Kolind has seen to it that it's snowing sheet music in that tube every day.

Kolind's bold move shook up Oticon. The crutch it had been leaning on was suddenly gone. The company had to stand or fall on its own. It stood tall. People realized they didn't need all that paper. They had a far more valuable resource: their own creativity, which was fomented through conversation in creativity initiatives, in project teams, on the staircase, online, and in the coffee bars. Kolind set the example, skeptics turned into believers, and the snowball started its roll. Such faith in the power of creativity is crucial to successfully revitalizing a culture. As Jerry Welsh, former head of worldwide marketing at American Express Travel Related Services Company, puts it, "The most important precondition for creativity is to believe in it. If you believe there is a big idea, then you as a manager are apt to want to find it. If you do not believe in Santa Claus you are not going to sit under your chimney on Christmas Eve. If you don't believe in Santa Claus, when he comes in you won't see him."

Belief also begets discipline. Weekend musicians can belt out some sweet tunes, but the greats practice every day. The same goes for companies. If you're satisfied with mediocrity, hey, feel free to have a creative burst now and then before quickly settling back into a deadening routine. But don't be surprised if your company falls right off the new global map. Today's great companies live and breathe creativity. They work doggedly to coin the alchemy of imagination and innovation that leads to great products and services year in and year out, just as a rust-belt factory spews out widgets on an assembly line. You may walk into a jazzy, happening company and think: *These people are having too much fun*. Don't be fooled: All those people are working very hard. But they're having a great time because their creative juices are flowing, and their work has meaning. That charged and playful atmosphere doesn't simply materialize. Savvy managers, who send a constant, consistent message that they value creativity, work assiduously to devise an environment that ignites everyone's enthusiasm. Creativity becomes a process, not an event.

M. Douglas Ivester, president of the Coca-Cola Company, puts it this way: "You need to make creativity the norm and the lack of creativity the exception, as opposed to trying to take a company and say, 'Well, we're going to be creative this week.' You will be creative that week, but it will be totally irrelevant. It's important to establish an aspiration of creativity. If you go to any sort of meeting here, whether it's finance or marketing or technical, that aspiration, that expectation, is going to pop out. It'll just overwhelm you. That's what's inside people's heads. And it's what we preach to them." Coca-Cola has created this climate of creativity through ceaseless reinforcement. Top management reiterates its commitment to out-of-the-box thinking at every opportunity. From the factory floor up, everyone is encouraged to come up with innovative ideas. Newsletters, discussion groups, and suggestion solicitations drive home the message: This self-renewing giant values creativity.

Perhaps I've convinced you that companies like Coca-Cola and Oticon provide desirable work environments. Now that you're enthusiastic you're probably wondering about the right way to proceed. It's wise to go forward with some caution. After all, everyone knows that the invariable reaction to change is resistance.

If your company has been plodding along for years with a stodgy, hierarchical, rigid culture, don't expect the change to be one big lindy hop: be-bop-bop, and suddenly everyone is dancing to the same tune. Creative cultures threaten as well. Let's, for a moment, switch from the 1950s to the 1750s. Remember Salieri and Mozart in *Amadeus*: a modestly talented man's toxic envy of a great genius. A creative culture values talent and the courage to take risks. Those who lack these qualities often envy those who possess them. Envy, though, isn't the greatest enemy of an innovative culture. Fear is a far more pervasive obstacle. People may be afraid there will be no place for them in this hot new dance.

You must address those jealousies and fears. A company

intent on creativity must let all its people know that they are valued for their individual strengths, and that the whole is much greater than the sum of its parts. Obviously, some people are more talented than others, but *everyone* in your company has creative energy. Let people know you appreciate that energy and want to tap into it. That's what it's all about: bringing out the best in people. Go for it.

You can often overcome fear of change by expediting the change itself. When it's over, and the sky hasn't fallen, you can almost hear the sighs of relief. Sit down with people. Let them know what you're doing. The unknown is what most scares us fragile mortals, and we will make up whatever explanatory stories we need about the what, why, and how based on prior history and personal perspective. If someone continues to resist what you're trying to do and drags down the creative balloon with carping, well, show that person the door.

In your swift housecleaning, you must ruthlessly trash outmoded obstructions to creativity: standard operating procedures, protocols, norms of behavior, a confining brand image, rules, the revered memory of old successes, and so on. This is always difficult; it obliges people continuously to revise their sense of themselves and their place in the organization. Human frailty is the issue here. You must couple your bold action with education and sensitivity.

Creation is always a struggle. Struggle is part of the process, and that struggle strengthens the end result. A creative culture values give-and-take, friction and argument. A jam session is a polemical interaction of instruments, a conversation. That's the kind of tension you want your corporate culture to encourage. Some players rise to wail the clarion call of change. Others sound the horns of alarm.

How else are we to test the resilience of the creative proposal? You want to create a forum to find the perfect balance between art and discipline, today and tomorrow, inspiration and nuts and bolts. Getting real is risky, not to mention expensive. There must be a low-cost means of testing the value of new ideas, and there is. The natural antagonism of fear and courage can become a tool for measuring an idea's validity. And it's your job as manager to create an atmosphere that encourages free thinking and risk-free expression, and transforms antagonism into creative energy.

But watch out. It's easy to get caught up in the excitement of change, and it's perhaps even easier to lose sight of your goal—a culture that encourages and cultivates creativity at all levels. You'll have to fight the easy answers to begin the real transformation.

One all-too-common mistake is the confusion of the word "creation" with the activity. If I had a grand for every company that says it fosters creativity and innovation, I would be a billionaire today. It's almost as if these talk-the-talkers think that if they mouth the words—presto chango!—a wondrous world of creativity will magically appear. Give me a break! To shape a culture in which creativity flourishes, you have to build it into corporate strategy and systems and live it every day. Check your commitment level before you start pontificating. Hold meetings. Make sure you have support at the top (and bottom). Put together a blueprint of specific actions. Devise twenty concrete cultural changes you're going to make. Start making them. Then—and only then—open your mouth and start crowing.

A creative culture is an open book. It discloses its inner workings to everyone—not just to the elite. It describes precisely the kind of creative accomplishment the company aims for, as well as its strategic importance and the behavior required to achieve it. This openness suffuses company communication: from annual reports, advertising, and public relations, to the ways managers relate to workers, to human resources's systems and training—in short, all the formal ways in which dialogue in a company occurs.

Many companies try to capture their culture in public statements. Stressing its high-performance leadership model, PepsiCo lists thinking outside the box—defined as "creat[ing] opportunities and overcom[ing] obstacles by rethinking or reconceptualizing the business"—as a core competency for managers. A good manager "creates new and unique approaches to resolve problems. Understands the larger picture and uses its broad perspective of the business to constructively challenge usual ways of seeing things . . ." Well said, indeed. It's not surprising that PepsiCo has been wildly innovative and profitable for so many years. It doesn't simply spout creativity, it has put its own stamp on the definition and lives it.

Shiseido Company, a Japanese maker of high-quality cosmetics, medical products, and food products, often speaks of its "higher purpose . . . serving society": helping people age healthfully and beautifully. The company codifies its creativity mission on laminated plastic cards that employees carry around in their shirt pockets. Examples of Shseido's "twelve steps" of creativity include the need for focus, the value of finding inspiration from nature, and the importance of curiosity, accurate observation, and fun. Heavily oriented toward technical and scientific research, the company places great emphasis on creativity in its culture and encourages employees to regard their creative work as a contribution to personal self-esteem and contentment.

But realigning a company's culture to foster creativity is an undertaking that may tax your ability to maintain equilibrium. As the crusty corporate culture crumbles, questions arise. Should internal competition be encouraged or downplayed? Is there a point at which creative abrasion becomes counterproductive, and, if so, what is that point? Is excessive judgmental review inhibiting originality? How can you promote a meritocracy without triggering an anti-elitist reaction? Accept these questions: They're a healthy sign. But resist the urge to settle for easy answers. We live in a Technicolor world. In this complex age, very little is black and white. There is, rather, a lot of gray—and red, orange, yellow, blue, and so on. Every company must wrestle with such decisions within the framework of its own unique structure and strategy. You must handle these tough questions— you got it—creatively.

Where does the tidal wave of new technology fit in as you foster your creative culture? First of all, it adds new capabilities with which your folks can play. A potential danger, however, of all this technological wizardry is that it can remove people from the intimacy of direct human contact.

That's why the empathetic aspect of a creative culture is so important. High-tech doesn't change human nature or the human need for the confirmation, reassurance, and guidance of personal interaction. On the contrary, "touch" is increasingly important in deconstructed and virtual organizations. The creative culture might be thought of as "high touch"—an anchor that ties each individual to the group and conveys a comforting sense of solidarity, even among people who don't work face to face. This is similar to the function of the retail stores of primarily mail-order businesses like Sharper Image and Victoria's Secret. A good initial anchoring experience gives customers a sense of ongoing connection to the business when they order from a catalog. Bottom line: Technology is a wondrous, creative tool, but to get the most from it we must skillfully integrate it into the creative culture.

The responsibilities of top leadership in effecting cultural change include generating vision and enthusiasm and providing resources and support. Most senior people in mature corporations work at some distance from the sources of creative ideas. At that level, leadership's job, says Peter Roth, a Polaroid senior project manager, "is not to come up with the answer, because they are too far removed from the problem. It is to promote an environment that will solicit answers from all levels because good ideas come from anywhere." This demands "a courageous openness": a sense of self strong enough to recognize that one doesn't know all the answers. This admission that he or she is human is often hard for the I-am-God school of CEOs. Cop to it, people: There are some problems even almighty you can't solve. A creative culture can't flourish in an autocratic environment. Period.

Managers are at the front lines of an organization's cultural renewal: They translate those lofty visions into day-to-day actions. This is where the rubber meets the road. Do their acts support or contradict the company's stated commitment? How managers interact with people—especially how they talk to them—is crucial. In the end, after everything is e-mailed and networked, it's the good old spoken word that matters most. Although business gurus have said relatively little about managing through conversation, everyone who has ever held a job knows that the informal exchange, the ad hoc snippet of advice or instruction, often carries more force than memos, handbooks, or directives. Encouraging words, tone of voice, facial expression, body language: Those are management's most powerful tools for inspiring people and are intimately connected with culture. You seed confidence and creativity by being confident and creative, and you project your substance loudest and most clearly in person. And conversation, as we have seen, can be facilitated by physical places as with Oticon's shrewd design of its headquarters, with its lounge areas, coffee bars, and casual work-floor arrangement, to encourage easy dialogue.

Jamming, of course, is inherently a kind of conversation. It's the improvisational element in jazz, where one note bounces off another, and no one knows where it's all leading. That sense of possibility, of spontaneous dialogue, is a crucial element in the creative culture. Michael Serino, research fellow at the Lotus Institute, describes the founding of Lotus's internal think tank, as a "series of conversations." Richard Saul Wurman, information architect and creator of the TED Conferences, describes the power of dialogue as coming from "saying something new to a single other person, opening up possibilities."

Communication is the essential medium of a creative culture: the communal sea in which we all swim. Mastering its nuances is the surest path to success for a manager seeking to implement a culture in which innovation and imagination thrive. A company that can't communicate is like a jazz band without instruments: Music just isn't going to happen.

Let's break down this crucial skill into components:

1: *Creativity is a two-step.* A manager's first priority is to allow ideas to develop by keeping possibilities open. It may be the second, third, or even fiftieth idea that clicks: Keeping the process open and avoiding premature closure are crucially important. Because creative work is exploratory by nature, it deserves suspension of disbelief in the early stages. Bottom line: Reserve skepticism and doubt until assessment time. Creativity embraces the paradox of needing to keep communication open and nonjudgmental with the ultimate need for measurable results. In that sense, it is a two-step: You push, you pull; you step forward, you step back; you maintain an atmosphere of openness, and you judge, always with sensitivity to the ongoing flow of the process.

Polaroid's Peter Roth sees the goal as being unafraid "to say something that someone else might call crazy. Don't prejudge it. Think about it." Consider, especially, pieces of an idea that won't work as a whole. "Don't be totally judgmental immediately after an off-the-wall idea. It may have some seeds of useful concepts. If you accept the premise that everyone may have the seed of a very good idea germinating somewhere within, that attitude needs nurturing and a grass-roots effort."

Jerry Welsh, formerly of American Express, states, "Here is the way we handle ideas in our organization. We have the same hierarchy as every other company. When your employee gives you an idea, you must always distribute it no matter what it says. You may comment or not comment. You may send it on with this note: Joe has just sent me an idea. I am confused. I am against it. I am horrified. Whatever you say, you pass it on. You ought to be free to have bad ideas because at least 90 percent of your ideas will be bad if you have enough ideas to have good ideas; bad meaning not dramatically impactful, too expensive, too destructive of the culture, too illegal, too risky for the business, plain wrong-headed. You ought to be free to have bad ideas. That is not the same as feeling free to implement a bad idea and therefore to fail."

2: *Positive-speak inspires confidence.* While filming *Indiana Jones and the Temple of Doom*, Harrison Ford offered some suggestions about how he and another actor should block out a certain scene. Director Steven Spielberg—as shown in a documentary about the making of the film—didn't seem overly enthusiastic about Ford's idea, but he took care not to reject it. "I like that a lot," he said. "Let's just explore one other option." Spielberg's choice of words is significant. He uses the phrase "one other option" to achieve what he calls, elsewhere in the documentary, an "opportunity to double and redouble ideas." Spielberg does not seem to judge, evaluate, or criticize at any point in the process. Positive-speak preserves the climate of openness to ideas. You wound no one in the process—even when you chose a path radically different from what another person has suggested. A manager who shuts down communication by being critical or judgmental is left with the authoritarian option alone.

3: *Discover the gold nuggets in the muddy stream of ideas.* When you offer negative feedback, you should take care to weave it into a positive reaction to the work as a whole. "You try to find the positive," explains Jon Craine, Polaroid's director of corporate design. "Even if it's something you think is bad, you can find positive aspects. And you can weasel in your own ideas." Retired Polaroid vice chairman Sheldon Buckler asserts that managers must recognize the value of creativity and make it their mission to create a climate that fosters real creativity. "We want a strong statement in the company that we value creativity and that it's a priority." Straight negative feedback is a great way to stifle creativity and choke innovation. The 3M company goes to great lengths to provide a creative environment with stability. Employees enjoy corporate recognition of their achievements, which the company encourages with an atmosphere that stresses freedom. Charlie Prather, former director of the Du Pont Creativity Innovation Center, emphasizes the value of a positive, open forum: "You have to allow people to get out the ideas they came to the meeting with—let them be heard and honored—before you go on."

4: *Your schedules, timetables, and deadlines should harmonize disparate work styles.* Synchronizing differing perceptions of time ranks high among human problems. Creative people often scoff at tight schedules and deadlines, whereas a manager inevitably must acknowledge their reality. When a project falls a week behind schedule because the manager hasn't procured the right logistical support, the creator is horrified. When the creator is an hour late to a meeting, it's the manager's turned to be shocked. The job of negotiating a mutually satisfactory agreement about time is part of the manager's job.

Not long ago, the CML Group, a noted retailing company based in Acton, Massachusetts, worked with Richard Altuna, a designer famous for arriving at meetings late—sometimes on the wrong day entirely. Altuna's habits didn't change, but team managers, recognizing the importance of his contribution, learned to overlook his tardiness, even when he showed up on the wrong day. Exceptional people sometimes need exceptional boundaries.

5: *Well-set boundaries define extensive possibilities.* All the same, productive life is impossible without *some* boundaries. All organizations need to gauge the constraints of their limited resources, pressures of time and competition, and other factors that circumscribe the creative effort. A great measure of managerial skill and flair is the ability to maintain accountability to the company without removing the fizz from the creative champagne.

The truth is that many creative people appreciate controls and even rely on them. Artists from Michelangelo to Jackson Pollock understood artistic creation as an act of balancing imaginative freedom with technique and the limits inherent in a given medium. The immortal jazz pianist Bill Evans said that jazz was free "only insofar as it has reference to the strictness of the original form, and that is what gives it its strength. There is no freedom without being in reference to something."

6: *The rhetoric of creativity can lay bare the crux of profound puzzles.* Managers need to develop a rhetoric of awareness, persuasion, diplomacy, and resolution. The goal is genuine dialogue, dialogue that leads to an explosion of ideas. Try to pose questions that return the discussion to the state of the beginner's mind. Toyota uses its highly regarded technique of posing the five whys: You ask a question, get an answer, then ask why. Do that five times, the Japanese say, and you will understand the essence of the situation. You will have broken through a superficial understanding to reveal the more fundamental issues. Skillful managers of creativity know how to pose questions that stand problems on their heads. Or they approach them from an unexpected angle. Or they change their basic terms—any one of which may spark an epiphany. At Meiji Seika, the art of asking the right question is considered to be an explicit management skill.

7:. *You are dealing with individuals—not interchangeable parts.* The creativity manager must be a kind of diagnostician or detective, using exploratory questions about "big" matters to gain a much-needed sense of team members' personalities. Spielberg's direction, as he works with a detail-oriented set designer, an emotional actor, and an enthusiastic cameraman, reveals him to be a veritable "linguist" of the creative psyche. He addresses each person individually, in his or her own idiom. This master director also displays a detailed knowledge of every aspect of moviemaking, and his expertise inspires confidence.

Spielberg in action illustrates a key principle of managing creativity through conversation. One person needs detailed instruction. Another needs only a word to the wise. Another needs praise all along. Others are scornfully proud and manage best with no praise. And others value praise only if it includes honest critique. But be cautious. Though you can type every person as one sort or another (usually several), people always resent being categorized. F. Scott Fitzgerald's advice to writers is valid for everyone, including managers: Search for the individual, and you will get the type. Search for the type and you will get . . . nothing. Every individual has his or her own psychology. Thus the masterful creativity manager is part psychologist, able to speak each person's unique personal tongue.

Warning: Managers lose credibility when their vocabulary is off and they betray their ignorance. If you don't know what someone's talking about, ask. For God's sake, ask! Learn the language of the creative subculture. Making that effort demonstrates your respect, and respect will win you confidence and trust.

The heart of fostering a creative culture is communication. Culture isn't about machines or numbers or logistics: It's the all-encompassing ethos of a company. And it can succeed only if you promote it—whether through informal chats or plastic tubes that cut through the middle of a cafeteria. You must seize any and every opportunity to create a culture of imagination and innovation. Write down twenty ways you can bring the commitment to creativity alive in your company. Be creative.

RIFFS

▶ Success depends on your ability to infuse, imbue, and instill a respect for and belief in the power of creativity throughout your company.

▶ It's useless and hypocritical to spout a lot of talk about creativity and then retain processes that deaden the imagination and spirit.

▶ Savvy managers, who send a constant, consistent message that they value creativity, work assiduously to devise an environment that ignites everyone's enthusiasm.

▶ You must ruthlessly trash outmoded obstructions to creativity: standard operating procedures, protocols, norms of behavior, a confining brand image, rules, the revered memory of old successes, and so on.

▶ You want to create a forum to find the perfect balance between art and discipline, today and tomorrow, inspiration and nuts and bolts.

▶ Imaginative leadership must sustain enthusiasm with words that guide and inspire.

▶ A creative culture cannot flourish in an autocratic environment.

▶ Jamming, of course, is a kind of conversation . . . That sense of possibility, of spontaneous dialogue, is a crucial element in the creative culture.

▶ Learn the language of the creative subculture. Making that effort demonstrates your respect, and respect will win you confidence and trust.

7

CRAFTING THE CHALLENGE

Managers are increasingly being called upon to exercise self-reliance, flexibility, and imagination—that is, creativity. They're being asked to stretch and grow—to jam—to help their companies improvise in today's rapidly evolving global economy. It's all about challenges: setting them and meeting them.

Management is a performing art. Like teachers, like litigators, like film directors, like politicians, like generals, like coaches, the best managers have a bit of the ham in them. Or should have, if they want to build creative organizations.

One of the most famous *coups de théâtre* in recent business history occurred on the day a senior Sony executive paid a visit to his engineering department to challenge the ingenuity of the people there. Like a fairy-tale king visiting his alchemists, he produced a small rectangular block of wood and dared the engineers to design a tape player of the same size. "No bigger than this," he declared. The techies went to work, but soon came up against a seemingly insurmountable obstacle: They could not devise a speaker that would fit into such a tiny package. Then one of them had an intuition, inspiration, illumination, revelation, epiphany—whatever. He asked himself: "Why does it need a speaker at all? Let's do the job with small earphones!" Whereupon the Walkman was born.

In fairy tales, of course, the hero of such a story would be the person—a bullied youngest son or stepdaughter—who solved the puzzle and saved the day. Here, however, defying fairy-tale morality, I argue that the real hero is the king—the manager. It was he who "thought the unthinkable," as Oticon's Lars Kolind would say. A tape player you could carry in the palm of your hand, or in your shirt pocket, or strapped to your arm, or clipped on your belt. It was he, too, who had the panache to "present the unthinkable" in the theatrical way he did, using the block of wood as a vivid prop.

In the three preceding chapters, I have discussed three signature skills of creativity management—the mental (beginner's mind), the spatial (zoning for creativity), and the ideological (cultivating a belief in creativity throughout the organization). We have looked at clearing the mind, clearing the space, and clearing beliefs. In this chapter, I focus not on the techniques of stimulating the creativity of "others," but rather on the creativity of managers. The manager of corporate jamming knows how to use his or her imagination to prod, provoke, and inspire new levels of innovation and achievement. The manager creates the challenge that ignites the breakthrough.

This is a surprisingly touchy topic. Too many managers still see themselves as cogs in a system that tells them to be creative about as often as it tells assembly-line workers to be independent. At the same time, no manager—no person, for that matter—likes to be considered "uncreative." It's insulting, like being told you have no sense of humor or that you are "average."

But the traditional industrial system of production, as we saw in Chapter 1, is a lumbering dinosaur. The bureaucratic manager suited the needs of a time when complex manufacturing processes required unbending control. Managers' tools were the standards, operating procedures, and rules that promised unexceptional assembly-line production, in short, the sheet music. A routine was set, and it was the manager's job to keep it routine. This was acceptable in an era of predictable competition, steadfast investors, docile customers, and slow-footed change. That era is gone. Corporations today must live in a permanent state of mobilized awareness—of themselves, their performance, their customers, and their competitors. And, thanks to information technology, this is increasingly possible. Managers, for the first time in history, are being called upon to exercise self-reliance, flexibility, and imagination— that is, creativity—as part of their ongoing job description.

They're being asked to stretch and grow—to jam and boogie with a new managerial mindset—to help their companies improvise in today's rapidly evolving global economy.

It's a demanding new world. For example, a by-the-book, middle-aged middle manager may perceive an almost unbridgeable chasm separating her from a twenty-four-year-old software designer wearing six earrings in his left ear, who, while he programs his Silicon Graphics reality engine, subsists on a diet of dried peas and Pepsi. Who do you suppose will be shown the door: the narrow-minded manager or the groovy genius? After a successful career, earning the rewards of the old system, the old-style manager finds it difficult to loosen the reins; the American landscape is littered with the psychic corpses of these unfortunates. What American business values in today's economy is knowledge, imagination, talent, innovation: creativity. Old-style managers never expected that someone might change the rules behind their backs, and now they're in the difficult situation of having to change horses midstream. This is the challenge they face, and their struggle to redefine themselves as creative catalysts merits the support and encouragement of corporate America.

On the other hand, the new era doesn't ask managers to create what artists or scientists or techies create, only what managers (and only managers) can create: cost-effective, sustainable environments for productive and creative work. Managers are the integrators—the supportive, flexible tissues—that connect beliefs to goals, culture to strategy, performance to reward. They energize their people and make creative work possible. Sticking with our musical metaphor, they manage the record label. They define the overall "sound" of the enterprise, generate a terrific environment, establish standards of quality, bring in great people, provision creative efforts with needed resources, and establish boundary conditions such as budgets and schedules.

But once again I risk hitting a raw nerve. For managerial creativity—leadership—is as sensitive a topic as sense of humor. I mean, of course, the kind of leadership by challenge shown by the legendary Sony executive. We would all like to think ourselves similarly capable of mobilizing our group, team, division, or corporation, but secretly, I suspect, most of us wonder if we'd succeed. Such effective theatrics, we believe, are strokes of luck, or of genius, beyond our limited repertoires. In this chapter, however, I'm going to dispel those doubts. I'm going to show that almost all managers can carry off leadership by challenge. And, in the current business climate, they must.

Let's look at several companies that successfully meet the creativity challenge:

▶ At 3M, managers are an integral part of that innovative company's creative energy. They regularly organize internal trade shows that let different departments share one another's brainstorms and inspirations. The result of the cross-pollination of ideas is a perpetual state of challenge—a vigorous spirit of creative competition. It was in 3M's culture of challenge that Art Fry invented Post-its. Today, to stimulate continuous innovation, 3M aims to have young products—no more than five years old—earn at least 25 percent of its annual profits.

▶ The CEO of manufacturing giant AlliedSignal, Lawrence Bossidy, makes a habit of leaving headquarters for frequent visits to Allied facilities. He gathers groups of some twenty employees—no name tags, no ranks, no bosses—for informal lunches called skip-level meetings at which he challenges them to improve the company's operations and profitability, and to speak openly and freely. One result: Two frontline factory workers at AlliedSignal's Tempe, Arizona, aerospace-parts manufacturing facility redesigned and shortened—from five days to two days, and, ultimately, to two hours—the process for moving raw materials from loading dock to production line. Thanks to their ingenuity, AlliedSignal has already saved millions.

▶ Microsoft Corporation is arguably a creative—and successful—company in the current business landscape. And Bill Gates has fashioned a company whose creativity is shaped by an ever-renewed challenge. Bill Gates himself is the main avatar of challenge. And the culture at Microsoft is constantly about raising the bar. The talent of Gates and his designers is the foundation of the Microsoft phenomenon. But managers play a crucial role. As the conduits of the company's dynamism, they infuse life at Microsoft with the spirit of challenge, constantly restating and renewing the challenge in fresh ways. They mold the often-chaotic business of creation into workable, achievable goals. Routines, per se, do not exist for a Microsoft manager: Managers are creative partners.

From such new paradigms, legends—the parables and folk tales by which a community teaches and reinforces its customs and spirit, its ethos and ethics—are born. Legends—embellished, retold for years and years—give mythic status to history. So it happens that the people of Sony have mythologized that block of wood, that the people at Oticon still talk about Lars Kolind's think-the-unthinkable memo, and that at AlliedSignal the two women who took up Bossidy's challenge and redesigned the raw-material cycle time emerge as folk heroes. Those legends are about people who created, molded, and met the challenge of creativity. The legends themselves perpetuate the impact of the managerial challenge.

How does a manager, on a day-to-day basis, create that challenge? This is where the art of stagecraft comes in. You want to surprise people? Shake them up. Grab their attention. Make them think, dream, and jam. Props—like a block of wood—work. Outrageousness, too, works. Consider the Coca-Cola executive who began a meeting by asking all the people there to imagine that they had just been laid off—better yet, to imagine why they had been laid off. Or Jan Timmer of Philips, who printed a newspaper datelined in the future that announced the company's bankruptcy. Or the strategy blueprint Lars Kolind drew after he went off by himself to ponder Oticon's conversion from a prosperous bureaucracy to a creative (and even more prosperous) dynamo.

Business schools don't teach us how to use those elements of stagecraft (although perhaps it's time they start). Managers who hope to thrive in today's new corporate climate would do well to take a class in stage direction. In theater, the director's role includes integrating the work of the creative team (writers, actors, and designers) with the production team (stage manager and stage crew) and the business team (producers). The director defines the dramatic vision and the boundaries of the creative act. Using actors, sets, costumes, lighting, and props, the director manipulates the audience's perceptions. During the rehearsal process, the director prods, provokes, inspires, and challenges the actors or designers who feel stuck or stymied. Using the unexpected, and even the outrageous, the skillful director controls the impact of the drama.

In business, it's the manager's responsibility to craft a coherent challenge. The clarity and precision of that challenge inspire and expedite the creative process. It was John Kennedy's injunction to put a man on the moon by the end of the 1960s that led to the space program and its eventual success. To craft an effective challenge, a leader may invoke metaphor. Bausch & Lomb uses the notion of the greenhouse to denote the process of product development—ideas grow with careful nurturing in a controlled environment. Louis Gerstner, as president of American Express's Travel Related Services Company, used the four-minute mile to represent company aspirations: He wanted his company to move to the front of the pack with record-breaking speed. Metaphors are important because they not only stimulate the imagination, they appeal to the emotions. Metaphor—more appealing than pure rhetoric—gives vivid life to a challenge, transforming the intangible into an image people can more easily grasp.

This, then, is the creativity manager's own great challenge: Find and use the language, props, and stagecraft to fashion an inspiring challenge that reflects the company's larger goals. Challenges are risky. People both hate and love a challenge. Their reception of your challenge will depend to a large degree on how you present it. When Jimmy Carter gave his infamous "malaise" speech, challenging Americans to come up with a "moral equivalent of war," he was only expressing a widespread and very plausible opinion. The country had just suffered the shock of Watergate, the rude awakening of the oil crisis, and the pain of defeat in Vietnam. "Malaise" was as good a word as any to describe the nation's fallen spirits.

Yet somehow it was the wrong word—disastrously wrong. And despite its impeccable origins in the works of William James, America's most American modern philosopher, "moral equivalent of war" was wrong, too.

Historians still debate the reasons for Carter's failure to craft an effective challenge. Some maintain that the time wasn't yet ripe. Others argue that Americans will never find language like Carter's acceptable. We want our challenges voiced in positive terms, not as vague psychological ideas like "malaise," which carries with it the hint of disease or weakness. Look at Franklin Delano Roosevelt's legendary "We have nothing to fear but fear itself." What a brilliantly framed challenge: reassuring, uniting, holding promise of a better day, and inspiring what is strong and good in all of us.

The goal is to craft a challenge that resonates. The trick for every leader is to find a motivational metaphor for the organization. The metaphor implies a language as well as an icon, or set of icons, that integrate thought and feeling. The challenges become three-dimensional, existing in words, images, and deeds. The metaphor enables comparisons and linkages between the literal reality around us and the figurative reality of the imagination, of the emotions and of intuitive possibilities, of dreams and the ability to dare to dream them.

In my travels, I have met a number of people who intuitively and expertly craft a challenge that is resonant for a group of talented people. Consider the following examples:

▶ Francis Ford Coppola's direction of the epic film *Apocalypse Now* provides a literal example of how to craft and stage a challenge. Coppola could have, much more easily, filmed his Vietnam-era epic in a safe, accessible tropical venue such as Hawaii. Instead, he chose to transplant cast and crew thousands of miles away, to the jungles of the Philippines, where guerrillas were actually engaged in war. "This was the first directorial decision: to put people in the situation of the film," Coppola explains. Talk about framing and staging a challenge: Actors, designers, and crew had no choice but to work harder, dig deeper, and use every ounce of their creative juices. The result: a great film.

▶ Many of us know about the recent history of the Scandinavian Airlines System (SAS) and the role of the charismatic Jan Carlzon in its turnaround. Carlzon transformed the airline from a technology-dominated bureaucracy to a customer-obsessed company run by empowered frontline personnel. But few have fully explored one particular facet of this success story: that Carlzon called on a notorious symbol of the Chinese Communist state, the Cultural Revolution, to serve as a model of corporate change.

　　The parallels between the Chinese and the SAS cultural revolutions are many. By turning the organizational pyramid upside down, Carlzon transferred power from the elite to the frontliners, just as Mao had earlier sent the political elite to plant rice and perform manual labor in the countryside. Mao's strategy focused on educating the vast population of China while eschewing academic and expert knowledge. He advanced that Herculean project with his Little Red Book, a compilation of knowledge of every sort—from military strategy to community organizing to the proper relations between men and women. Published as a waterproof paperback, it was for a time the most popular book on the planet. Carlzon produced SAS's own little red book—a volume of cartoons and text designed by a Stockholm advertising firm—that communicated all aspects of the company's strategy in a simple, easy-to-learn format. Initially people dismissed that book as patronizing, but the scoffing quickly turned to admiration when they realized that for the first time everyone was working from the same playbook. Once Carlzon determined the core metaphor, the rest followed, and he was able to reenergize a company that had previously spent too little time worrying about people. Carlzon had brilliantly framed and crafted a company-wide challenge: Put customers first.

▶ Finally, let's return to the example of Lars Kolind. His efforts at Oticon are a paradigm of how to craft, and then stage, the challenge of creative change. It is notable that Kolind went off alone into the hills, so to speak, to write his now-classic think-the-unthinkable memo, for the redesign of the company. Why? Because at the time, as he points out, no one in the company shared his sense of urgency about the challenges facing Oticon. After writing his memo, Kolind recruited key lieutenants to his cause. He then embarked on an effort to spread the challenge company-wide. He held meetings at which he dared everyone to rise to his challenge. He laid out the scenario: Think the unthinkable, and then discuss, argue, and debate. Kolind instituted bold changes: He cut paperwork, and walls literally came down. He abolished job descriptions. He enjoined managers, designers, and frontline employees to follow his example and come up with new processes and products. With the memo, Kolind crafted the challenge, and then he went on to stage it.

While he accepted a certain amount of chaos and difficulty with the process, Kolind established limits. He defined what he would and would not do. At one point he finally stated, in effect, "This is the deal. I am going to do it, and you can decide whether to do it or not." His tone was challenging without being confrontational.

Kolind caused a lot of confusion. A middle manager was quoted as saying, "All of a sudden we did not know what to do. We did not know what our jobs were all about, and it was a very tough time for us. You had to position yourself in the new organization. You had to create your job again, in a new context, with new relationships. Lars told middle management that we were going to be almost obsolete in the future, that we were going to change the company from a management-driven to a project-driven organization. For some managers, it was very unclear for a long period what they should do. They felt really lost. Nobody made an attempt to tell them what their job should be in the future: That was part of the process. They were purposely left alone by Lars Kolind—to sort out people, to see if they were capable of working in a different environment and could be part of a dynamic and flexible organization." Kolind was willing to accept this chaos in the interest of change.

What makes Oticon's story so compelling is the way in which Kolind integrated, that is, orchestrated, the elements into a compelling piece of music. Once he had defined his core ideology—think the unthinkable—and the crucial need for creativity and speed, the rest followed: the physical architecture, the paperless office, human resources practices, hiring, decision making, organizational structure (or rather the destructuring of the organization), and finally, the addition of information technology to the mix.

The results were striking. No one left the company, and that stability made for a rapid return to profitability.

Here are seven aspects of a well-crafted challenge: language, context, mouth and money, preparation, discipline, complicity, and empathy.

1.   LANGUAGE

The very nature of a challenge demands careful crafting, if not in JFK's "high style," at least in vivid language. We want to deliver our challenges in full costume, rhetorically and visually. Anything less and we begin to doubt the seriousness—both the gravity and the earnestness—of the challenge.

Kennedy put everything he had into his speech exhorting us to conquer the moon: his own charisma, the eloquence of Ted Sorensen, and the grandeur and stature of his office. Challenge is an act of aggression. (Why else would we speak of "capturing" an audience?) And the aggressor risks appearing not just a failure, but a ridiculous failure. Hence the need to state your challenge with absolute clarity.

Eckhard Pfeiffer, who was named Compaq Computer Corporation CEO in 1991, was given a mandate to put the company back on track and regain the market share it had lost to such competitors as Dell Computer and Gateway 2000. He decided to work backward: Rather than calling for his people to design and build a computer, calculate costs, and finally set a price, he phrased a counterintuitive directive. He challenged the product development staff to "design to price." The result: In 1993, Compaq's new computers shocked the competition by selling nearly twice as well as the year before.

2.   CONTEXT

A challenge you issue out of the blue will go nowhere. Kennedy voiced his challenge in the context of America's Cold War rivalry with the Soviet Union. The Russians had put a spaceship—a manned missile, in effect—in orbit around the earth. Were we going to let the USSR outshine the USA? No way.

The business world, with its inherent dynamic of competition, provides no lack of critics to the mere rhetoric of challenge. Moreover, managers today enjoy a rhetorical advantage that was virtually unknown even fifteen years ago. They can count on each employee's intelligence and savvy. Unlike their parents or even their older siblings, today's workers and managers are "business literate," wiser in the ways of global corporate competition, subscribers to the business publications that used to go exclusively to the executive suite. They are better prepared than ever to listen to sophisticated messages.

Eastman Kodak Company named George M. C. Fisher as its CEO in 1993. For years, the company had, in its effort to preserve its high margins, consciously relinquished overseas market share to Fuji, Canon, Sony, and other competitors. When he joined the company, Fisher, who was quick to note the emergence of the global economy, pronounced a new regime: the reversal of that situation. "You don't," said Fisher, "sell market share. That is religion with me. You don't have a business in a few years if you keep doing that." And his senior executives understood that his challenge held them accountable for reaching the company's goals.

3.   MOUTH AND MONEY

There must be consonance between the status of the challenger and the seriousness of the challenge. By that measure, Kennedy was well placed. Long before the idea entered JFK's head, scores of others had raised their voices in favor of "going to the moon." Today, for that matter, powerful lobbies campaign on behalf of America's "mission" to lead the world to Mars. But no one paid, or pays, attention to them. To be effective, challengers must have the "right" status:

They have to be in a position to put money where their mouths are.

Kennedy, obviously, was in such a position. Managers must take care that they are, too. It's no good challenging your team or division or company to rise to your daunting challenge unless it's clear you can and will provide the resources and support your people will need.

As an example of mouth and money, at IDEO, the state-of-the-art San Francisco–based design firm, every employee has access to more than half a million dollars' worth of computer equipment to help spur creative inspiration. 3M is only one example of a company that uses pools of slack money to pursue blue-sky projects.

4.   PREPARATION

JFK's man-on-the-moon challenge was not an act of impulse. He pondered his every word to determine its effectiveness and possible consequences. Creative leaders in business must also take care as they prepare their challenges. When you ask people to commit time, energy, emotion, and soul, think through what you're doing before you act.

Creativity is born of experience. Don't jump in with both feet unless you know where you are headed. The recognition by Virgin Atlantic Airways that it was in the full-service transportation business inspired a limousine service for its business and first-class passengers. Once Virgin's managers perceived its larger calling, they knew what to ask from its employees and from themselves.

5.   DISCIPLINE

Undoubtedly the most compelling element in Kennedy's 1961 challenge was the time element—the commitment to a deadline. America would not simply put a man on the moon; the country would do so in just eight years.

When people condemn "rhetoric," what they mean is "empty" rhetoric, words without commitment, sincerity, or enthusiasm. That's why all successful challenges are to some extent promises—promises of resources, of moral support, of personal participation, and of accountability. Such promises warrant the challenger's commitment and the significance of the challenge.

In the modern age, no commitment is more persuasive than one that acknowledges the clock and the calendar. A promise to meet a deadline commits you to a thousand other promises: You will devote your mind, energy, anxiety, physical and human resources, money, politicking, and more.

As stagecraft, there is nothing like a deadline—a countdown—to capture your audience's attention. The convergence of promise, time (or boundary) limit, and challenge creates a community. Look back at the etymology of *ethos*, *ethnic*, and *ethics*—that is, of our spirit, our community, and the basis of our morals and customs—and you will find they all derive from a notion of place, locality, territory. Well, that's what deadlines do: They put boundaries around a group of people, thereby giving them, along with discipline, a sense of community to make it meaningful.

At Philips Electronics NV, top executives meet in

"Centurion" sessions to compare company products and strategies with those of the competition. Senior managers critique—frankly, sometimes brutally—one another and their superiors, imposing a sense of urgency that catalyzes creative solutions to apparently time-sensitive crises. With no sacred cows, no taboo topics, the discussion becomes a festival of fast-forward thinkers.

6. COMPLICITY

Without saying it in so many words, JFK let us understand that he, the challenger, had challenged himself as well as his audience. Ethics alone dictate adherence to this rule, but managers who fail to observe it will suffer more than reputations for hypocrisy. Their authority will collapse, and they will fail.

Steven Spielberg carried his chair on the set of *Indiana Jones and the Temple of Doom.* Richard Branson writes in his black notebooks to signal the importance of ideation in the business process. And M. Douglas Ivester is fond of making anonymous storechecks and bringing insights about selling opportunities back to the corporate mainstream of the Coca-Cola Company.

7. EMPATHY

Finally, the leader of creativity challenges through his or her humanity. This involves the art of empathy. Leo Castelli, the legendary art dealer who nurtured the careers of such modern masters as Robert Rauschenberg, Jasper Johns, and Claes Oldenburg, referred to his artists as "my heroes." He is a noteworthy practitioner of the simple acts of kindness that make the difficulties of creative work easier to bear. His generosity—providing financial stipends for his artists, helping them with dentist bills, and the like—is well known.

Empathy encompasses appreciation of the difficult creative process. Bo Goldman, who wrote the screenplay for the film *Scent of a Woman*, says, "Creative work is hard. When you get successful, then the work becomes harder. And the pressure gets harder and harder with the studio and others. You're fighting for your work all the time. And to them, it's shoes. They are selling shoes." And *they* are managers, who are too often correctly perceived as enemies of the creative process. Brian Frankish, executive producer of *Field of Dreams*, states the cardinal injunction to managers: Remember the crucial importance of "making the creative person comfortable." What does that mean to managers? They must stay loose, improvise, and look for empathetic ways to present their positive challenges.

Effective leaders focus continuously on renewal, on raising the level of dissatisfaction. Lars Kolind took it upon himself to redesign Oticon at a time when no one else perceived a problem. Duane Roth of Alliance Pharmaceutical describes his role as "simply every once in a while to change the path a bit." Tom Tierney, president of Bain & Company, describes his role at the company as "handing out hunting licenses for ideas." It's the role of the leader to bring in the new agendas, to add new grist to the mill, to inject the unexpected, to create variety and new relationships, and whenever possible, to delight.

Keep everyone a little off balance. It's a dance that Michael Laude of Black & Decker describes as "constantly pushing to say that this is not good enough, try this the other way. You have to balance it, push a little bit, and then back off a little bit."

Management is a demanding responsibility in today's chaotic new era. Rules are often obsolete before we've recorded them. Leadership poses two big challenges: one internal, managers crafting challenges, and one external, managers staging challenges. The two are always closely related. It's not that complex. Creativity, at its very core, is often simple: as simple as a block of wood.

RIFFS

▶The creative manager—the manager of jamming—knows how to use his or her imagination to prod, provoke, and inspire new levels of innovation and achievement. He or she creates challenges that ignite breakthroughs.

▶Corporations today must live in a permanent state of mobilized awareness—of themselves, their performance, and their competitors.

▶Managers must create cost-effective, sustainable environments for productive work. They are the integrators—the supportive, flexible tissues—that connect beliefs to goals, culture to strategy, performance to reward. They energize their people and make creative work possible.

▶The legends of corporate triumphs perpetuate the positive impact of the managerial challenge, giving both the challenge and the triumph of meeting that challenge status throughout the organization.

▶ It's the manager's responsibility to craft a coherent challenge. The clarity and precision of that challenge inspire and expedite the creative process.

▶ There are seven aspects to a well-crafted challenge: language, context, mouth and money, preparation, discipline, complicity, and empathy.

1. Language: Deliver challenges in full costume, rhetorically and visually. Anything less, and we begin to doubt the seriousness—both the gravity and the earnestness—of the challenge.

2. Context: Challenges you issue out of the blue will go nowhere.

3. Mouth and money: There must be consonance between the status of the challenger and the seriousness of the challenge. To be effective, challengers must have the "right" status: They must be in a position to put their money where their mouths are.

4. Preparation: When you ask people to commit time, energy, emotion, and soul, think through what you're doing before you act.

5. Discipline: Successful challenges are promises— promises of resources, of moral support, of personal participation and accountability. Such promises warrant the challenger's commitment and the significance of the challenge.

6. Complicity: Challengers must let the members of their audience know that they challenge themselves to succeed at the same time that they dare the audience to pick up the gauntlet.

7. Empathy: Empathy encompasses appreciation of the difficult creative process.

8

THE PERPETUALLY CREATIVE ORGANIZATION

Recruiting outsiders to "sit in" and jam—perhaps on a just-in-time basis—on specific projects has become common in business. Like jazzmen, outside musicians who sit in and shake up a tired tune, these migrant virtuosos are never more essential than when in-house creativity flags.

William Gibson set his remarkable sci-fi novel *Count Zero* in a world where nations no longer fight wars over territory. Empires no longer war over ideology, nor do ethnic or religious groups fight over political correctness. In Gibson's world, it is corporations that wage wars for the services of gifted people. The particular object of contention in *Count Zero* happens to be a biotechnologist, but it might as well have been a software designer, a basketball player, an artist, or a brilliant financial or marketing strategist. Sound improbable? Think again. Such struggles are not just the stuff of fiction. Companies go to war every day to win the services of the gifted and talented. The primary weapon of corporate choice is money, but prestige, perks, affiliation with peers, access to resources, and promises of creative freedom are also in the arsenal.

Still, this is hardly late-breaking news. We've always relied on the accomplished and precocious to unearth and solve the world's puzzles. Colonists mounted the American Revolution at least in part because of their determination to industrialize textile manufacturing. Trouble was, even after they won the right, nobody knew how to build the mechanical loom, the hardware needed to do the job. A group of American merchant bankers, led by John Nicholas Brown, solved the problem by luring a remedy to Rhode Island: Samuel Slater, a British mechanic, carried the designs in his head to New England. Four hundred years before, Renaissance princes had contested bitterly over the services of great artists such as Leonardo da Vinci. And almost eighteen hundred years earlier than that, Philip of Macedon was proud to persuade Aristotle of Athens to serve as tutor to his son Alexander, soon to be "the Great."

And only recently, IBM paid well over $3 billion for the

intellectual property of Lotus Development Corporation: property that appears to reside, for the most part, in the head of Ray Ozzie, designer of the powerful networking software, Notes, and his hand-picked team. The fact is that genius has always been in demand, has always been in short supply, and has always had its price.

Through the generations, institutions—monarchies, merchant banks, baseball franchises, corporations, and the like—waged the competition for genius. The artists and mechanics, athletes and philosophers were essentially transients. They came and went as the occasion, the project, or the whim of the patron dictated. There was no question which side had the decisive power: The artist or genius served at the pleasure of the patron.

In today's global economy, however, transiency characterizes both sides of the deal; the relationship between patron and genius is more impersonal, and the balance of their power is closer to equilibrium. But it's even more important to our discussion of creativity in organizations to note that competition for exceptionally creative people is now a fundamental, unavoidable, do-or-die factor of business success.

What's driving this revised equation? A new "culture of the temporary" is in the making here. Recruiting outsiders to "sit in" and jam—perhaps on a just-in-time basis—on specific projects has become common in business. Like outside musicians who sit in and shake up a tired tune, these migrant virtuosos are never more essential than when in-house creativity flags. As piano player Billy Taylor says, "A man faced with the kind of challenge you get in a sitting-in session is not so prone to imitate. He's apt to concentrate on building better and more original solos."

Astute company managers of today know that it is up to them always to maintain a fountainhead of creativity—a continually renewable source of ideas. Some have recognized that the minds of ingenues are where the freshest insights, like jazz riffs, originate. The Coca-Cola Company, for example, recently hired 150 new marketing people. None of them brought prior soft-drink industry experience. Jan Timmer made sure that not one manager involved in the change process at Philips Electronics had direct knowledge of the area he or she was responsible for. Peter Roth of Polaroid has said, "Sometimes an expert may be the worst selection to solve a problem. It may come from someone outside who has no foreknowledge or training in a particular area and therefore may come up with the most unique and creative solution."

Michael Stern, formerly of General Magic, speaks of such maneuvers as "throwing salt into the solution to make it gel." General Magic works with large companies that are looking to develop new products but whose senior executives seek a partner in formulating a vision of the future or in executing that vision. Stern says, "They need an outside catalyst to focus their approach to the markets and to give them the tools to work with. They can't fight battles on their own turf unless they have new tools and outside relations. What we offer is fresh ideas and the tools to execute them. And the combination is what matters. There are lots of fresh ideas. There are lots of marketable technologies. The trick is to put the two together."

Organizations that once seemed like the pyramids—built for the ages—are now playgrounds for creative professionals who move in (after a good offer) to run a project and leave with the project's conclusion or when work elsewhere looks more appealing. A vital organization is one that is forever jamming—inviting the invention of fresh perception.

Corporate power is also shifting toward boards of directors, whose allegiance is itself shifting from the CEO to the money managers in New York, London, Tokyo, or, for that matter, Omaha, Nebraska. This power is related to the revolution in electronic communications, which has reduced power's ancient inhibitors—time, distance, and ignorance—to negligible incidentals. The increase in the density of information flow has created more efficient markets. More efficient markets mean that investors and other stakeholders in organizations are more insightful about the risks of doing nothing and about the imperatives of creativity. Every morning of their ever-shortening tenures, CEOs and their entourages awaken to the clarion call from the financial pages: "So, what are you going to do for me today?"

Tough as it is, there's no better way to direct the managerial mind to creativity. That's what investment capital wants: And what money wants, it gets—or else. This hasn't always been the case. Investors once perceived creativity as risky. Of course, those were the days when investors could reasonably expect business as usual to provide a very decent return on capital. Nowadays, whatever the risks of creativity, they're nothing compared to the risks of stagnation. It would be an exaggeration to say that all investment capital today behaves like venture capital, but it's no exaggeration to say that it wants to. It certainly wants even venerable enterprises like IBM to act with the sprightly inventiveness of a startup. The pressure is on, folks, and it's only going to get turned up.

Of course, there's a lot more to it than the money managers' profits-or-perish edict. Creativity is a company's most promising long- and short-term investment and its path to getting and staying anywhere near the top of the greasy pole known as the global economy. Management must relentlessly cultivate an environment of enthusiasm for creativity, even beyond the need to respond to pressures from investors who are better informed than ever before. Management should take its cue from investors' ravenous appetite for creativity—either home-grown or purchased on the open market.

Note that we're talking about acquiring human creativity here, as opposed to *creations*—novel goods or services. This is as true for a company already teeming with creative resources as it is for a firm with little or no in-house creative capacity. There are three ways to get what it needs. It can buy innovative companies, hoping that their creative people will continue to generate new and profitable ideas. That's what IBM did in its acquisition of Lotus. Or it can cut a deal with hot companies, short of outright purchase, to share the fruits of their creativity. The alliances between large drug companies and their small biotechnology counterparts, like SmithKline Beecham and Human Genome Sciences, is just one prominent example. The third option is to scour the countryside for creative people and try to establish an alliance with, befriend, rent, or consult with them. Though this is probably the most common strategy, it's also the diciest. Creative people lose steam pretty quickly when you force them to fit into a deadening corporate environment. You cannot simply install creative people without first ironing away the bureaucratic wrinkles that can reduce the experience to a frustrating disaster for everyone.

Before a company sets out to master the new rules of the creative marketplace, it must first understand the principle of *free agency*. Free agency, which the sports world introduced to the rest of us, rages through every skill market: academe, high-tech and biotech think tanks, corporate and foundation leadership, and entertainment industries. A free agent is always on the lookout for a better gig—better money, better people, greater impact on society, more freedom, more opportunity for personal growth. To further complicate matters, not only are performance stars free agents, publicly held companies are also up for grabs, and their owners are generally more than delighted to sell out to the highest bidder. Until recently, investors were in for the long haul; so were management, labor, customers, vendors, and local communities. Over time, however, the twin imperatives of capital growth and creative freedom have loosened the ties joining people, places, and institutions and given rise to a culture, or even cult, of the temporary.

It's not surprising that Hollywood is the best place to watch this pinball game in action. Ed Bleier, a senior executive at Time Warner, told me that the entertainment industry has pioneered this new business model, since film companies reinvent themselves for every movie they make. An entirely new cast and crew assembles for each production. This new model emerged only after the collapse of the classical studio system in which the Hollywood studios were custodians of scarce expertise in all aspects of movie finance, production, and distribution. In fact, those early "dream factories" were vertically integrated empires, as hierarchical as the big businesses that produced tractors and soap powder. Long-term contracts controlled actors, writers, and directors, slotting their time into tight schedules as if their talents were just so much raw material. Paramount, Loew's, Fox, Warner, and RKO also owned chains of movie theaters where their products had exclusive runs. Thus did the majors dominate an intrinsically creative industry: They controlled the most important talent, which they developed and nurtured, and they owned all its outlets.

With a little help from the antitrust laws, the whole Hollywood system disintegrated. Stars, in particular, realized that they held the ultimate power: box-office appeal. Studio hierarchies dissolved like so much Kool-Aid. Studios today are banks, managers of distribution channels, and purveyors of scarce technical expertise, while the creativity resides in the world of the independents. Creative people scattered in all directions, free agents at last, while the "suits" became, in effect, investment bankers for independent productions. What arose from this seeming anarchy was a harbinger of the culture of the temporary—a culture that is in full flower throughout the business world today, as the battle for the gifted has escalated to full-blown war. And who are the generals in this war? Agents and other intermediaries such as venture capitalists. They drive up the astronomical sums talent now brings. In this era, even cinematographers and sound men and women have agents. Jim Carrey wants $20 million? No problem. How about $5 million for a software designer? Here's the check. A mere $50 million to lure that brilliant CEO? Hey, she's worth it. Here is the new system. No creativity inside, big creativity outside. Guess what, big company? You need to act like today's version of a Hollywood studio. You need to know how to get talent to want to work for you. You need to manage your relationships. Because a studio is only as good as the creative talent it has a relationship with at any given time.

The same truths increasingly apply across other industries. The "stars" call the shots. They refuse to tie themselves down. There will always be another dynamic little company that comes up with a product or service that captures the nation's imagination and pocketbook. Whether it is pharmaceuticals or construction, large companies are increasingly acting like studios. And those that aren't had better learn the lessons of creativity if they want to attract talent.

Consider today's biotechnology industry. Fifteen years ago, there were no more than a mere handful of American biotech firms. Genentech was the best known. By 1994, venture capital had backed some thirteen hundred startup companies. There are three arenas for biomedical science in the United States. The vitality of the first, academia, is increasingly compromised by funding cutbacks. The second is corporate. Although companies such as Merck & Company and SmithKline Beecham PLC spend billions each year on research, their approach tends not to be cutting-edge. In fact, only a few of the major pharmaceutical companies still include avant-garde research as an integral part of their strategy. What's more, their creative people work in regimented corporate laboratories stiflingly similar in structure to the old Hollywood dream factories. That problem is particularly acute in Europe. One senior scientist, after he'd resigned from a prominent Swiss pharmaceutical company, described his corporate life as "a charade of paper shuffling" that bore no resemblance to actual science.

The third area, comprising venture-backed biotech companies, is where the action is. Most of these companies, which may or may not have external scientific advisory boards, sprang from the scientific breakthroughs of one person or a small creative team. The hope, of course, is to turn those insights into viable products.

Why are these biotechnology companies flourishing? In a word: creativity. These are dynamic places that nurture and inspire scientists to chase their visions. These folks don't want to be stuck in a constricting corporate environment. Attracted by freedom (and the chance to reap financial rewards), today's scientists are more willing than ever to gamble their careers on small new companies. Venture capitalists, the agents of biotechnology, often play an important role by bidding up the price on these scientists, using stock options as the lure.

It's not only on an individual level that this freedom and creativity are appealing. Bringing a new drug to market is extremely expensive: The necessary research and clinical trials can easily consume $100 million to $200 million. Therefore, many small companies establish alliances with major players, who contribute the attributes of a studio: a brand name, financial backing, and a wide range of development and resource capabilities. The pharmaceutical giants, for their part, are happy to cough up the huge ante it takes to win the small companies, their fresh air, and their new ideas. SmithKline Beecham pays $125 million to Human Genome Sciences, a company whose only asset—it won't have a product ready for a decade—is a collection of brilliant scientists.

What we're talking about here, really, is a substantial revision of what defines a corporation in the age of smart, nimble, fiercely demanding creative investment capital. The corporation itself is now a source of this capital. Scouting networks are already in place, designed to bring small, creative enterprises to the attention of large, rich, and not so obviously creative ones. Take the Global Business Network, a company that specializes in matchmaking. GBN links its large corporate clients with one hundred of the best creative minds in business, the arts, medicine, and the social sciences. An outgrowth of Royal Dutch/Shell Group guru Pierre Wack's notion that scenario planning is better conceived of as "a party with remarkable guests" than as an analytic study, GBN creates an independent forum that invites clients and members to exchange ideas, creating a marketplace of ideas in which companies looking to create their futures are exposed to leading-edge ideas and people.

First Virtual and Bain & Company both encourage the loyalty of their alumni. Each sees value in supporting a network of former employees who can augment the firm's awareness, provide leads to new opportunities, and even return to the fold as returned employees, partners or advisers. First Virtual explicitly assumes that its employees will only stay with the company for a finite time; it is looking for a rapid turnover to provide a constant influx of new perspectives and creative abrasion. At the same time, it looks to its alumni as important resources for launching new entrepreneurial initiatives under its corporate umbrella. To provide the "glue" that encourages loyalty, Bain makes its proprietary computer database available to its alumni and alumnae, who are free to roam the company's virtual spaces in search of information on companies, contacts, business intelligence, and new methodologies. It underscores the belief that once employed by the firm, you are always considered part of the family, and that its responsibility to you extends beyond the term of employment.

Worldwide managers of investment capital—relentlessly scanning the globe for new sources of returns—are at the bottom of a great push for creativity in business. That financial thrust is a part of a larger phenomenon, sometimes called the "collage" effect of modernity. We now understand that our business institutions—financial entities as well as producers of goods and services—are ongoing projects pasted together to respond to whatever challenges, opportunities, and dangers we face. The result, in the business world, looks nothing like the corporation as we've known it. Rather, as the great French and American painters of the 1920s clearly saw, it's an animated, three-dimensional, ever-revisable collage—like Matisse's famous paper cutouts.

And in the realm of music, of course, as those same artists saw, the result sounds like jazz.

RIFFS

▶ Talent has always been in demand, has always been in short supply, and has always had its price.

▶ Competition for exceptionally creative people is now a fundamental, unavoidable, do-or-die factor of business success.

▶ Companies go to war every day to win the services of the gifted and talented. To do battle, the corporate weapon of choice is money, but prestige, perks, and promises of creative freedom are also in the arsenal.

▶ The twin imperatives of capital growth and creative freedom have loosened the ties joining people, places, and institutions and have given rise to a culture of the temporary.

▶ A company with little or no in-house creativity has three ways to get what it needs: It can buy innovative companies, hoping that their creative people will continue to generate new and profitable ideas. It can cut a deal with hot companies, short of outright purchase, to share the fruits of their creativity. Or it can itself scour the countryside for creative people.

▶ Attracted by freedom (and the chance to reap financial rewards), today's creative talents are more willing than ever to gamble their careers on small new companies.

9

CYBERJAMMING

The Internet culture is a jamming culture. It's nonhierarchical and centerless. Its forms and formalities are purely occasional, opportunistic, experimental. Like jazz, it is profoundly democratic and egalitarian.

The creativity age is upon us, we've said, because that's where the floodtide of information technology wants us to go. It's now time to back up this assertion.

As Charlie Parker had his "woodshed," I have my kitchen table—the Kao venture sushi bar, as one wag dubbed it. It's where I form new companies, plan conferences, prepare speeches, conceive courses; I can easily wipe it clean, and the nearly paperless table is quickly ready to support my next deal. My equipment consists of a high-end personal computer, a speakerphone, a state of the art videoconferencing system with groupware, and a high-speed Internet connection.

I can do a lot with these tools. I can bring collaborators in on deals, and, as we share information, we sculpt virtual teams. Databases can be searched. Complex documents can be drafted using templates of my own design to help me organize the process of doing deals. But those instruments of business invention are only on the frontiers of usefulness: We haven't seen anything yet.

I often imagine what it will be like in five or ten years. Perhaps someone calls to ask me to develop a particular new enterprise. When I sit down to work at my kitchen table, it will take me only minutes to make the necessary trademark search, background research, competitive analysis, and financial model. I can get the legal documents I need almost instantly. Intelligent agents generate the documents digitally: Lawyer-on-a-Chip, a service of leading law firms, provides clients with the right legal advice exactly when they want it, in other words, just in time. These digital, lawyerless encounters are remarkably quick and pleasant.

As a cyber-entrepreneur, I then digitally scan my list of colleagues, friends, and associates for likely collaborators in the proposed enterprise. Another search locates potential investors, who, mindful of the press of competition for opportunities to invest in creative ideas, may respond with dazzling speed. They may have encoded their investment parameters digitally so that I can easily scan for investors' fit with my particular opportunity. A cybernetic agent combs databases for market information that would take an Olympic-level human researcher months to compile. I prospect for experts, advisers, directors, and managers who might be interested and available. With all the data I assemble, it takes little more energy to prepare a business plan and pro forma financial statements. All this without getting out of my bathrobe. In this future, people will lay the foundations of new enterprises at warp speed instead of months or years.

"Transformation" is an overworked word these days, but no softer one will do to describe the marriage of human creativity and information. Technology has enabled us to generate knowledge that leads to the discovery and exploitation of new business opportunities. Information technology is a powerful new instrument for jamming. Let's look behind this assertion, to see what it really means.

Cyberspace, according to John Perry Barlow, cofounder of the Electronic Frontier Foundation and occasional lyricist for the Grateful Dead, is what's at the other end of the wire. It's where you go when the phone connection is made, when the modem howls. More important than where cyberspace is, though, is what goes on there. Jamming is the what. The Internet culture is a jamming culture. It is nonhierarchical and centerless: Its forms and formalities are purely occasional, opportunistic, experimental. Like jazz, it is profoundly democratic and egalitarian, a competitive/cooperative meritocracy of talent. Anyone can converse with anyone else.

Interactions are consensual. The trappings of status are irrelevant. Cyberspace is a jazz club for ideas, open all day and all night, with the universe for walls.

Information technology confers leverage to creativity. By abolishing the advantages of scale, it has leveled the competitive playing field. It overturns the conventional wisdom that knowledge is power. It's really creativity, amplified, that creates that power. That's why Barlow can say: "The technology is so powerful that being big is increasingly meaningless. We're on the verge of an era in which you can start a multinational corporation in your garage." Technology provides a powerful amplifier for creativity.

Although it's pervasive, cyberspace is not necessarily a mass medium; quite the contrary. Entry to cool digital meeting places will seem like virtual reenactments of the scenes outside Manhattan's hot discos in the 1980s. Access to this world, despite the democratic aspects of electronic exchange, will become increasingly competitive. Entry to desirable areas of cyberspace will require special skills, renown, money, prescience, or other distinction. Passwords will be the talismans of the new software. There will be trailer parks as well as Malibu beachfront property in cyberspace.

In that world of tomorrow, we can imagine new tools for the creativity woodshed, cybernetic agents that will help creative people to get their thoughts into digital form and represent their interests around the clock in a variety of virtual marketplaces. We can imagine new collaboration-enhancing tools for the bandstand. Renault's Yves Dubriel has made much of his ability to quantify idea generation through technology in the contributing parts of the Twingo team. He said once, "Building a car like a Twingo is several thousand creative decisions," and he was known to check in with teams

whenever he sensed a decline in their rate of idea generation. It's only a short step to cybernetic tools that enable the
detailed representation and monitoring of creative process.

This new wave of technology is extremely important for
the future of business creativity. Creativity management is
often an elusive process. But watch what happens when
you take a geographically dispersed, expertise-diverse
product development team and put everyone in a collaborative groupware environment such as Lotus Notes. This
turbocharges creative interaction, giving way to a new
level of jamming that consists of themed conversations,
institutional memory, knowledge representation, and
group learning.

It also introduces what Ikujiro Nonaka and Hirotaka
Takeuchi, Japanese management and innovation gurus,
have called a hypertext organization. To me, this is an organization whose structure and culture can be configured
and reconfigured in a flexible, opportunistic, experimental
way, depending on vicissitudes of the creative project with
which it's charged. The hypertext company *is* its projects,
each one layered on top of the others, not effacing them,
but leaving them in the form of "texts" for future reference.
It's the sum of its ideas, knowledge, and capabilities, as
well as—at the most fundamental level—its bricks and
mortar. Oticon is a hypertext organization, a business that
disproves the old adage that you can't rebuild a ship at sea.
In the hypertext organization, the rebuilding includes not
only the ship's design, but its workings and ports of call,
with project overlaid on project for as long as will and
imagination last.

For me personally, working in cyberspace already offers
the chance to cast a gossamer electronic net over whatever

assortment of resources I may need: information, people, infrastructure, finance, alliances, and ways of defining the problem. In many companies, hard-wired organizational boundaries, structure, culture, codes, templates, and modes of interaction set problems in stone. In cyberspace, the tap of a key can reshape or dissolve those structures entirely. Boundaries in cyberspace, like Japanese shoji screens, are no more than paper-thin walls that provide structure but are easy to move, to change, to peer around. This allows us to commence a creative project free of the limits that define traditional approaches and historic concepts. In other words, form can truly follow function.

For example, as I write these words, I am also involved in an information technology venture that aims to create a digital network linking the one thousand member companies of the World Economic Forum, a major Geneva-based foundation. My team is highly dispersed: My design team is in Boston, certain advisers are in San Francisco, we are contemplating alliances with companies in London, New York, Atlanta, and Tokyo. Our customer base stretches around the globe. To manage this project, we are putting everybody on a videoconferencing system that is based both on Lotus Notes and on the World Wide Web. It would be impossible to mesh every participant's schedule requirements for physical meetings, but in cyberspace I can define a virtual meeting space where everyone's access to one another's intelligence and to our collected resources is unconstrained by time or place. We need to develop a business plan and technology, but we *don't* need to sit in a room together to achieve those goals. Drafts of our documents race electronically among us, and although members of my team are often unavailable by phone, they are easily reached via groupware.

Cyberspace is here, all around us, but we're still apprehending its significance, as generals do their next battle—through the lens of the last. Some people misjudge Lotus Notes and other forms of groupware, for example, as merely e-mail on steroids. But groupware offers so much more than that. It takes us a giant step closer to the brave new world of multimedia workgroup technology. For companies that want to set up their own private cybermeeting places without making a hefty investment in groupware, the Internet's World Wide Web provides an economical, powerful, and increasingly popular alternative.

The creative company is already wired for progress. The creative effort progresses in a nonlinear and iterative fashion. A company's capacity to consider ideas is limited only by the robustness and flexibility of its processes. Linear processes proceed one step after another, and, since the steps vary considerably in number as product complexity increases, many companies find themselves plodding into the future. For example, an old Hitchcock film called *The Thirty-nine Steps* turned on a spy's ability to memorize a complex industrial process comprising exactly that number of phases. Linear processes, even when they're efficient, set itineraries and specific routines, laying ambushes for new ideas. As each idea advances, it proceeds along a defined trail, much as if it were following sheet music or playing golf—as one has to—one prescribed hole at a time. Just as a false note or flubbed stroke can spell disaster to a player, so in traditional, linear-information processes, each misstep is potentially fatal.

Networks, however, are nonlinear: jazz rather than classical; musical basketball rather than musical golf. Networks function, like gifted leaders, in facilitating creativity: They are firm but sensitive enablers of public conversations. They put people in touch with one another and create unexpected linkages across established organizational boundaries. They champion processes that would otherwise, left to themselves, go nowhere. Information technology takes care of these functions at a basic level and thus permits leadership to focus on issues and concerns beyond the logistical.

In a world made accessible by the information superhighway, everyone has fingertip access to at least the entry level of high-quality information and expertise. Expertise previously available only through professional study and apprenticeship, guild membership, or an accident of heredity is waning in significance as a competitive factor. Such knowledge will soon be a mere commodity. The corollary is that creativity is *more* important than ever.

We will see the rise of many new forms of electronic networking. We will see situations in which scale is truly a disadvantage and in which advantage is a function of speed, instantaneous transaction, and the ability to make transactions happen: a deal-oriented mentality. Relationships rather than status in institutional hierarchies will anchor deals. We will see a wide range of infopreneurs arise: people who make fortunes from branded information, achieving the digital dream of making money while they sleep. I call these businesses Siskel and Ebert businesses.

What do I mean by that? Suppose Gene Siskel and Roger Ebert, the famous Chicago-based movie reviewers, open a kind of information lemonade stand on the digital highway. The moviegoer dials up and asks for advice about certain categories of films or for custom recommendations about movies playing either in theaters or on the zillion-channel, video-on-demand system of the day. Imagine that the charge for this valuable service is a mere quarter and that Siskel and Ebert field a million calls a day from the United States and abroad. The reviewers, whether their thumbs are up or down, whether they are awake or asleep, can earn enormous revenues. Rumor is, they've already started.

An entrepreneur with branded information—a gate-keeper to desirable data or opinion—will have the means to greatly amplify the value of that information and the effectiveness of its distribution. A whole new class of info-outlaws will also arise, untethered, nomadic, and grazing along the information highway. People who can manage a new economic model, who can set financial standards, who can develop their own versions of digital cash to reflect value are going to make a lot of money.

In addition, a new agent class of intermediaries will also arise. We have already commented on the significance of agents in the process of sitting in. Technology will also enable people on the creative side to enjoy an unprece-dented level of insulation. It can create anonymity as well as access. Agents will need to provide access and to make sure that talent's price floats to a market level. In William Gibson's world, everyone has an agent, even the data courier in the short story/film *Johnny Mnemonic*.

Such agents also guarantee reciprocity and ensure that transactions take place. In the old days, for example, in the Worldwide Chinese Business Network, clans and clan rela-tionships across the world sanctioned reciprocities. It was always possible, for example, even centuries ago, to send money from Hong Kong to, say, Singapore in the absence of a banking system, if a clan took responsibility for this transfer. Cyberspace dealings will require a similar tribal organization—extending the notion of "tribe" to a wide range of new associations and affinity groups—to serve as the intermediaries, certifiers, and insurers and to prompt the fingers to tap precisely the right keys. This function will be increasingly important in an era of private label currency and digi-cash.

Of course, by themselves, computers make no one more intelligent. Jon Craine, head of design at Polaroid, sometimes worries that his people "think the idea is going to come out of the computer screen, and it doesn't; I've seen them sit there and stare at blank screens. . . . I think we have to learn that the computer is a tool, not a substitute for creativity. Creativity still comes out of your brain."

But that tool so vastly increases the resources at one's disposal that change is qualitative, not merely quantitative. What are some of the dimensions of this change?

First of all, the information technology environment decreases the forces of friction. You don't have to wait at the library for the page to fetch your book from the stacks. You don't have to worry about lost information unless someone deliberately loses it. You don't have to wait for a scheduled meeting to get reactions to your idea. You don't have to wait for ideas to percolate through layers of bureaucracy. You don't have to wait to find the right person. Drag is proportional to drudgery, to the amount of back room administration that is required, to time delays, to organizational layers, and to organizational and team politics. Virtual organizations have a low coefficient of drag.

As a simple example, consider e-mail. E-mail messages reside patiently in cyberspace, awaiting the pleasure of their recipient. They eliminate the drag of the answering-machine, telephone-tag game. This "much more continuous dialogue" as General Magic's Mike Stern calls it, helps create a "new kind of intimacy."

Of course, computers serve us as seemingly limitless memory banks and tireless research assistants. Use of such tools helps mere mortals follow the fictional example of Sherlock Holmes, who tried to keep his head clear, and therefore ready for action, by never remembering unnecessary data for too long. Computers can erase useless information in a milli-second. How's that for generating beginner's mind?

Information technology decreases distance. It decreases the distance between customers and suppliers when they are linked together through electronic data exchanges. It decreases the distance between those who need services and those who supply them. It also decreases the distance between employees and contractors, allowing outsourcing in a more efficient and qualitatively different way.

In changing distance, information technology changes processes. For instance, marketing can be folded back on manufacturing or strategic planning. Linearity is no longer the central organizing principle. It also decreases distance in terms of the location of physical work. The new concern is work*space*, not workplace. Your Internet address is anywhere and nowhere, and, therefore, you can be wherever you want to be. Furthermore, your commute is over the moment you lift the cover of your laptop computer in the morning. The corollary is enhanced speed. Examples abound: Eastman Kodak Company is only one of many Fortune 500 companies that reports dramatic improvements in product development time due to successful linking of designers, toolmakers, engineers, and vendors on computer networks.

The new technology also enables diversity, which in turn leads to a higher quality of creativity. And we are speaking here not only of skills and experience, but also of the intimate level of cognitive style. Technology can help those who rely on intuition to keep track of the facts. Those who are data oriented will also find sources of inspiration. Technology can provide a *lingua franca* across business cultures, a way of bridging the gaps. A corollary is enhanced collaboration. Many have complained that technology distances people from one another, but it can also facilitate unmatchable, powerful, and far-reaching connection. It's a way to create membership organizations. It's a way to manage the invisible college of relationships among talent who may not work for you. And it's a way to protect subcultures within the organization.

If a measure of creative intelligence is the ability to make novel connections, then one form of increased resources for creativity is the greater availability of diverse input provided by information technology. The easy assembly of previously disconnected data, designs, ideas, and research findings— made possible by mere keystrokes on a computer—increases the chances that someone will see new connections among them and in doing so generate new insights and ideas. The clash of people with different specialties, perspectives, and interests that is facilitated by information technology also provides the means for technology-assisted arbitrage, for developing new knowledge in useful directions.

We have discussed these signature skills for creativity: clearing the mind, the space, and the beliefs. Information technology helps achieve each of these agendas.

The computer desktop metaphor is a huge success partly because we clear our actual desktops of the charts, drafts, notes, message slips, facsimiles, and assorted litter that accumulates over the course of a working day. We face the computer's blank screen with the clarity of Zen Buddhism's neophyte mind. The electronic desktop enables the person at the keyboard to feel he or she is starting anew, and with a fresh eye, unchallenged by the clutter of a working space, freed from the minutiae festering there, to see revelations. In short, the PC has, if you want it to have, a beginner's mind.

Information technology also permits clearing the space and creating instead a virtual project space. It uncouples work from a particular physical place, and locates it in a Platonic environment, freed of the hopelessly personal, idiomatic "rooms" we create in the real world. In that Platonic haven, in the realm of pure ideas, every time you boot up your computer, you make a space for yourself—an ideological, cultural, or "belief" space—where creative work can take place. And not only for yourself alone, of course: Cyberspace is as open to the creation of new forms of social life—subcultures in the making—as it is to new, individually generated ideas.

Information technology also enables interest and enhances awareness. It does so primarily by providing institutions with that great asset of a biological organism: retrievable memory. Memories make for wider, more diverse worlds. They increase creativity by letting us make new connections, by facilitating prototyping, dialogue, and knowledge sharing. This is also awareness on a continuous-flow basis, rather than information on a "publishing," on demand, model.

We obtain information in essentially two ways. Creative people in the grips of a hot idea can instruct their software to give them what they need, just as a surgeon requests a clamp. Information providers will deliver them the equivalent of a focused briefing worthy of the CIA or MI5. Other creative people, or the same ones when they're in the mood to do some intellectual touring, can go "web surfing," a form of scanning or prospecting in cyberspace, much like leafing through magazines or browsing museums, but on a technology-assisted, turbocharged basis. Doing this well—assembling random bits into a meaningful pattern or collage—requires learning a skill, just as does surfing in big breakers. Either way, touring or purposefully researching, the sheer quantity of ideas boosts our chances of achieving greater quality. The means for increasing the *results*—the production of new ideas—are much multiplied.

We will have the ability not just to search static databases, but also to encounter dynamic and qualitatively interesting sources of expertise through the use of cybernetic agents acting as amplifiers for our brains. Imagine a collection of "info deputies" scanning cities around the world for interesting events and reporting them on a network. That network provides the means for rapid feedback from other deputies who may have their own opinions to contribute. It will also enable us to carry out highly customized searches—say, for example, when a Japanese pharmaceutical company wants to know the reaction of European consumers to certain health products. Instead of sending a research team from city to city, the company will save a bundle of time and money by paying the network to obtain the information. They can have their results, literally overnight, if they have precisely informed the deputies of what's needed. Then they quickly can refine the survey results in electronic discussions.

Denmark's Oticon uses CM–1, a groupware standard by

which a dozen people can interact simultaneously on networked computers. That process eliminates the pitfalls of "real" meetings, which permit only one person to speak at a time and shape people's responses according to the speaker's status or the listeners' political ambitions. In virtual meetings of the type enabled by CM–1, any number of colleagues can "talk" simultaneously by tapping their thoughts on a keyboard into a common workspace. They can enter their comments on an anonymous basis, if they wish, so people can easily respond to an idea, rather than the person who came up with it. As used at Oticon, the system, and the company's online bulletin boards, are instrumental in a range of activities—from product brainstorming to evaluation of employees.

Walter Parkes, president of the film division of DreamWorks SKG, points to the organizational power of information technology when he observes: "What is interesting in terms of the architecture of knowledge is this: When I turn on my computer, I look at my icons. I see WP Personal. Then I see WP Group, and then I see Everybody's. There's my private stuff, my business stuff that is shared by my immediate group, and then another database that is for everybody." Shades of the woodshed, the jazz club, and the record label.

There is no longer any doubt that the volume of business transactions in cyberspace will continue to grow until computer-mediated collaboration achieves a critical mass. Recall that Metcalfe's Law says that the value of a network is exponentially proportional to the number of its users. At some point, enough hierarchies will have been transformed into networks, enough pyramids will have been flattened, and enough power will have been transferred from bureaucratic managers to nomadic entrepreneurs that our business ecology will have undergone a radical, qualitative change. We don't know when that will happen, nor do we know precisely how. We don't have a model for interactions in the Digital Age. We don't even have an idea about what skills we will need to manage in that environment. But it is certain that new kinds of organizations will emerge— enabling membership organizations, enabling jazz clubs. We will need new skills to assure trust and reciprocity in cyber-space.

The bottom line is that you won't have to venture beyond your keyboard to get in on the action. You won't even need a degree: You may well be working on your own. Writer William Gibson imagines a future world whose inhabitants are outlaws in the sense of living and working outside the old organizational structures. Everyone will be a kind of Me, Inc., trading and bartering information with a what-have-you-got-for-me-today? pragmatism. Outlaw or not, you'll be a decision maker—not a staff member or employee. And your kitchen table will be as good a place (or space) to work as any other.

RIFFS

▶ Technology provides a powerful amplifier for creativity.

▶ In cyberspace, we can define virtual meeting places where everyone's access to one another's intelligence and to collected resources is unconstrained by time or place.

▶ The creative effort progresses in a nonlinear and iterative fashion. A company's capacity to consider ideas is limited only by the robustness and flexibility of its processes.

▶ Expertise previously available only through professional study and apprenticeship, guild, or an accident of heredity is waning in significance as a competitive factor. Such knowledge will soon be a mere commodity. The corollary is that creativity is more important than ever.

▶ Drag is proportional to drudgery, to the amount of back-room administration that is required, to time delays, to organizational layers, and to organizational and team politics. Virtual organizations have a low coefficient of drag.

▶ The new concern is work*space*, not workplace.

▶ The easy assembly of previously disconnected data, designs, ideas, and research findings—made possible by mere keystrokes on a computer—increases the chances that someone will see new connections among them.

10

THE POST-INDUSTRIAL FACTORY

Warning: A business world charged with the freedoms and necessities of creativity is not a haven of peace and serenity.

Let me conclude with a speculation that is also a hope. My greatest hope for this book is that it will help create the business organization of the future—a factory of ideas. It will be a factory in the original sense of the word—an instrumentality, an agency that makes things. Of course, in the first and most important instance, the "products" of this factory are ideas, the music of today's world. And ideas are elusive, intangible. Their provenance is often obscure. They are also disturbing and divisive, pitting change agents against defenders of the status quo and requiring great courage to promote and test "in the full knowledge," as psychoanalyst Rollo May emphasizes, "that one might be completely wrong."

On the face of it, then, nothing could be more troublesome, more mutually inimical, than the notion of a factory that manufactures ideas. A factory, as we've known it in the Industrial Age, is the very model of a gritty, inflexible, non-experimental, anti-ideational human organization. A factory's business would seem to be forging plans and templates—the sheet music of production—into the hard-edged processes of an assembly line. A factory that jams? A factory that creates music online? Jazz music? Preposterous.

The idea of a factory also seems at odds with the process of creativity: a process in which not knowing defines the starting point. Not knowing is a fundamental reality of creativity, as many voices attest. Walter Parkes of DreamWorks says, "We're making everything up as we go along." Will Pape of VeriFone observes that the company has "always been an experiment in new ways of doing business." Carol Peters, designer of the Indy computer system for Silicon Graphics and CEO of software firm daVinci Time & Space states, "No single person here has ever done this before: We are trying to define a business role for ourselves that has never been played before, with a product that neither we nor anyone else has ever built before, in an industry that's still trying to give birth to itself." And Fred Bertino of the Boston-based advertising agency Hill Holliday agrees. "There are no beautifully cut paths," he says. "You have to be a bit of a bushwhacker—willing to take your idea and not let anyone stop you."

One of those most qualified to speak about business as discovery is Louis Rossetto. Rossetto cofounded *Wired* magazine, an initially unfundable enterprise that became one of the fastest-growing magazine startups in history. Echoing those themes of discovery, Rossetto states, "We are involved in exploration, discovery . . . We're like Lewis and Clark going out to discover what the Louisiana Purchase is all about. They didn't invent the U.S. west of the Mississippi, but they were searching to try to discover its dimensions, its topology, what lived there, what could survive there, what the dangers were, and the rest of it." This, for Rossetto, leads to a particular mindset. "What you need to be is very adept on the ground as you move into this space. You need to be able to take advantage of the weather and the terrain, so you know when to be carried along by a river or cut across it. You need to be nimble on your feet and open to new possibilities. Because it's so new, you don't know what you're going to discover out there in terms of predators and competitors. You don't know what is chasing along behind you until it catches up to you or passes you or comes at you from a different direction."

Rossetto is describing the antithesis of the traditional factory. And yet it's essential that we keep the old "hard" imagery of the factory along with the "soft" imagery of music. We must keep it not only because there is something inherently satisfying in the marriage of opposites—tangible and intangible, art and discipline, tonal and atonal, sweet and sour, grit and fluff—but also because in the business context, *those* opposites work together, or they don't work at all. We've got to have creative ideas and the value they represent. And, for all the business reasons—reasons of measurement, discipline, purposeful planning, efficiency at deploying limited resources, legacies of scale, and division of responsibility—we've (still) got to have factories. But we need to change their focus from mass production to continuous creativity. The apparatus of this factory will not be about physical machines as much as a mentality, a new managerial mindset expressed in relationships and in a new organizational climate. Again, it's about balance, about the two-step. Musical art alone—pure, spontaneous improvisation—doesn't cut it. That is, it doesn't cut records. After all, they do call it the music *business*.

Throughout this book we've seen idea factories in action. In the future, I see more of such companies, vying productively with one another in every industry, in every region, and in every country of the world. In fact, all companies will come to see themselves to a greater or lesser degree as idea factories. Some of them will be making more music than records: sounds without echoes in the marketplace. But all will live, work, and succeed according to the principle of interdependency: ideas dependent on successful products, successful products dependent on ideas, and both dependent on the effective management of creativity. Competition will be less about excluding the other guy and more about exploiting an aspect of interdependency—of being part of an ecological whole.

Managing creativity also implies mastery of certain skills. In my travels, I've met master practitioners of creativity, people who used a unique mesh of connections to put together something new, who were able to integrate the ingredients at a higher level, to see things more clearly, to make things happen with an effectiveness and lucidity that to ordinary practitioners would seem a bit miraculous. This level of mastery compares with the Zen chefs, whose knives grow sharper with every cut. In managing the creative process, there is, I believe, a real difference between competence and mastery.

Let's return to jazz. The beginning jazz musician pieces together bits of knowledge and imitates the solos of accomplished improvisers. Only much later does the musician begin to "play what he hears." There is a real difference between playing notes and playing what you *hear*. The skills are also about striving for simplicity and clarity. Bill Evans talks about the importance of playing things that are simple and true and, in the process, needing to play fewer notes. Those starting out, in his words, "try to approximate, but in a vague way. They do things in a way that is so general that they can't possibly build on that. If they build on that, they are building on top of confusion and vagueness, and they can't possibly progress. . . . It's better to do something simple that is real . . . something you can build on because you know what you're doing."

In addition, mastery is about moving from an abstract, intellectual understanding to one that is "in the bones," meaning integrated into one's worldview. It's easy for a jazz player to generate an improvised line based on conceptual, theoretical knowledge. But to play what one feels, from the heart, based on a given tune, and to have it coming out sounding *good*, is the most difficult art of all.

An important aspect of mastery is understanding the multifaceted nature of the competence required. Lance Nokumiru of VeriFone says, "If you're going to be a great company, you have to do it all. It's not enough to be creative if you cannot execute. It's not enough to execute if all you are building is something that people don't want. It's not enough to execute and be creative if you don't have the structures and culture to be viable long-term. You have to do everything these days if you are going to survive. The great companies out there do everything well. More and more it is becoming the case that people are getting good at all of the various parts. The pressure is really on." Mastery is about every facet of the dance.

What then are the elements of mastery? At bottom, creativity management is a matter of process skills as well as finding and developing a variety of spaces where *critically supportive listening* can take place. The factories I envision will house every conceivable sort of auditorium: from beginnings in the woodshed, to jam sessions in rehearsal halls, to performances in jazz clubs and concert halls, to work that takes place in the sound studios and testing rooms of the hottest record labels. These places will be filled with people who know how to play—more of them anyway than you probably imagine—and they will know how to listen to themselves and to one another. They will know, too, how to facilitate listening. They will set systems in place that will pick up the merest wisps of tunes. Then they will take those fragments and move them to the right evolutionary niche, giving them the right amount of time in space and the right-sized space in time.

Mastery also involves being able to go, not just from zero to one, to the creative result, but from one to zero, back to the beginner's mind. Great jazz musicians are humble. They are not attached to the process or products of creation. Guitarist extraordinaire Pat Metheny explains, "Every so often, you do get it right, and that makes it even more difficult. The standard to which you adhere keeps getting higher and higher." This is a poignant expression of the never-ending nature of the creative process: It's an exploration that is never finished—a journey that never ends.

The jamming that occurs in these idea factories will be less and less constrained by time and space. Picture the concert hall for the TED5 Conference in Kobe, Japan, 1993. Herbie Hancock plays a hot improvised duet on stage with Makoto Ozone . . . who is sitting in a Tokyo music studio several hundred miles away. Think of Frank Sinatra's duet albums for which the performances were recorded, for the most part, without Mr. Sinatra's ever meeting his various duet partners. These days the same thing applies to business jamming: More than ever before, we have the tools—in the form of computer networks and enabling technology—to jam over ideas without regard for the limitations of time and space. We can preserve creative heat while we vastly expand our creative choices.

We've said before that conversation is about jamming, about improvisation. Now we expand the point: Conversation is the organizational medium through which creativity is both expressed and managed. Michael Geoghegan of Du Pont once said to me, "The key competitive advantage of a company is who is allowed to have what conversations about what topics with whom and when." Business conversations are shaped by politics, hierarchy, structure, and systems; in short, by the sheet music. No wonder many organizations wind up talking to themselves instead of practicing the art of conversational jamming to create something new.

Companies can organize better conversations intentionally. Executive retreats are traditional opportunities for different kinds of conversations from those that we have at the office. Much of the corporate rituals of white-water rafting or playing golf is about creating new conversational opportunities. In Japan, the custom of taking your boss out for a night of dinner, heavy drinking, loose lips, and truthful conversation is well established.

But there can be a higher level of sophistication to the design of corporate conversations. Peter Schwartz, chairman of the Global Business Network, has described the art of "strategic conversation"—bringing together people from a variety of perspectives to converse about the future, much as players come together in a jazz orchestra to jam new themes. This is why Global Business Network includes members drawn from fields as diverse as physics, computer design, neurobiology, poetry, and rock music.

The pursuit of conversation, as we've seen, can lead to radical organizational redesign. Oticon is a prime example. In eliminating functional boundaries and structures, the company enabled conversations to take place across disciplines and functional lines, a process heightened by Kolind's metaphor of the spaghetti organization (everyone is connected with everyone else) and the multi-job (everyone does multiple jobs regardless of professional specialization). The emphasis on oral, informal communications over written memos was explicit encouragement to the quantity and quality of conversation. Conversations were also enabled by Oticon's open-plan office, a situation likened by Kolind to "being on stage"; it also illustrated Kolind's "birch forest" metaphor of moving people to where the work needed to take place (read: where the conversations need to take place). Oticon's project organization encouraged conversations whose intensity was stimulated by the temporary nature of each project-based working situation. Conversations were also enabled by clearing the space, down to specific architectural details such as the width of staircases.

Conversations are also enabled by information access. You can't talk about what you don't know. With very few exceptions, all information on Oticon's business performance and project organization is available to all employees via its online system. This is mirrored by the experience of the Global Business Network. In the words of Peter Schwartz, "Everybody in the company knows how much we've got in the bank, what we're billing, what we're owed, what we owe, and how profitable we are."

We have said before that information technology is the most important instrument in the creativity orchestra. This is in large measure because of its effect on conversation. The term "information technology" in this regard is probably inappropriate. Albert Bressand, of the French information technology think tank Prométhée, has advanced "relationship technology" rather than information technology as the appropriate term to describe the new marriage of computers and communications technology. The flexible reshifting of organizational boundaries enabled by the new technologies is the essence of the adaptable organization of the future.

This is the significance of cyberspace. It allows conversations to happen free of the limits of time and space. In the egalitarian jazz club of cyberspace, anyone can talk with anyone else at any time anywhere (if they know one another's e-mail addresses). Cyberspace becomes a meritocracy of talent, where players get up on a virtual stage to take their turn at "sounding good." And the technology is not sitting still. Cyberspace as conversational medium will come to full fruition when text-based online systems, the primary mode of cybercommunication today, give way to the multimedia communication that we glimpse on the World Wide Web as it prepares to explode on the scene in the form of full-blown, multimedia video and data conferencing services. Imagine being able to see your colleagues in high-resolution video anywhere in the world and to be able to have conversations supported by a variety of technical support tools such as document transfer and data conferencing.

Conversations need not even be linked to specific people located in a specific time and space. Being digital, to use Nicholas Negroponte's expression, can now extend to having conversations with digital representations of humans. In time, this technology will provide on-call intellectual sparring partners for the next generation of new ideas and open-ended conversations. Interactive voice mail and agent technology products coming onstream out of such companies as Wildfire and Agents Inc. are only a harbinger of the future.

At their heart, conversations allow us to create, since they are where divergence and diversity are realized. It is here that we can find the nonlinearity of creative leaps of thought, the ability to transform knowledge from data to insight, from insight to idea, from idea to value. And it is the role of leadership to encompass the valuable raw material of divergence by connecting people who speak a variety of emotional languages, often through . . . conversation.

Idea factories, like other businesses, will focus on culture and embed their beliefs in corporate-culture statements. But in those statements, creativity will be noted more explicitly and in far greater detail than in the past. Employers say they want innovative and creative people. This by itself is meaningless. In the future, we will spell out our demands for creativity with specific dimensions that define cognitive style, field of play, and rewards.

The cultures of these idea factories will vary tremendously, but they will all share certain themes. Among those themes will be a lack of sentimentality for the present order. In fact, an appetite for change as opposed to permanence will be the order of the day. Richard Saul Wurman, the noted and self-styled information architect, states, "There is only one question you can ever ask that has value: What would you do now if you were starting again? Life is what you do next. It's always next. Next is what it is. Next we can't do before, sitting here. Before is all over. All we can do is next. And the greatest of human emotions is anticipation of next."

In the idea factories, people will also know what they know and what they don't know. They will keep histories of their creative initiatives: where they came from, and how (or if) they were welcomed, criticized, evaluated, sponsored, stymied, realized, or put into production. The "map" of their company's creative resources will be as familiar to them as the organization chart was familiar to earlier generations of managers. And their map won't be the only one they consult and update: They will know their competitors' maps, too.

The idea factory of the future will have robust and lively links with its "outside" environment. Creativity management is to a great extent boundary management: erecting protective walls around fragile creations, punching windows and doors through the walls, and tearing the walls down altogether. And then, maybe, starting over. Thus, the architecture of the factory—and the rooms in it—will be in a state of continuous redesign, as though every manager had his or her own prototyping CAD-CAM device for organizational and managerial design and a ready willingness to use it. In this way, creative process parallels creative product. The temporary is the rule: Creative destruction is the order of the day.

The idea factory I have in mind is an exciting place, vivid and vital, and not just because it's alive with fresh thinking. It's exciting, too, because the tasks of management will have become as exciting as the task of invention. Invention itself will have become a management task. But beyond that, managers will also be called upon to play—and play well—a new and exciting counterpoint, a balancing act between openness and purpose, individual talent and group dynamic, safety and risk, play and calculation. Leaders will handle these paradoxes with aplomb, and they will handle the paradoxes in a manner that allows them to ask the right questions at the right time. To wit, the following refrain, in a different key:

Point	Counterpoint
Liberty	Discipline
Open-endedness	Purposefulness
Individual expressiveness	Group integrity

Safety	Risk
Beginner's mind	Professionalism
Playing	Calculating
Free form	Structure
Back to basics	Forward to the unknown
Etc.	Etc.

I am reminded of John Heider's injunction in his book *The Tao of Management*: "All behaviors lead to their opposites. Learn to see things backwards, inside out, and upside down." In other words, it's about the right issue at the right time. Sometimes we need more structure; sometimes less. Sometimes we need more professionalism; sometimes more playfulness. Sometimes we need to get back to what we know best; sometimes we need to clear ourselves entirely of preconceptions. Raising the right question at the right time is the skill of the creativity facilitator, and of the astute manager as well. Janet Axelrod, employee number one at the Lotus Development Corporation, says that the process of creating the company was "understanding how to do a dance, really that's all it is. You start moving your hips this way and your shoulders the other way. Fit yourself into the music, and make it work just right." Mastering this dance is about giving up the attachment to permanence, to certainty, to being in control, to playing from the sheet music. When you've mastered the dance, you no longer need to follow the markings of the foot chart on the floor.

In these factories of the future, I see executives leaving their corner offices to become catalysts for the creative resources of their organizations. I see laptops and mobile credenzas passing effortlessly through (physical) walls, charting new paths through (virtual) space. I see skeins of networked computers trawling the world for information, opportunities, and outside sitters-in. And at the same time they are setting the workplace humming with prolific, interconnected imaginations.

Finally, I see a growing division of (creative) labor in the global business ecology. As R&D becomes more expensive and risky, increasing numbers of global manufacturing giants—whether of cars, adhesives, pharmaceuticals, or widgets—will abandon whatever's left of their NIH (not invented here) creative pride. Like editors, they will become specialists in, and take their pride in, what I've called critically supportive listening: specifically managerial forms of creativity. They'll be expert at appraisal, finance, manufacture, marketing, distribution, and so on. But for the design of new goods and services, manufacturers will become increasingly reliant on sitters-in, outsources, allies, or talents from the world of independent production.

Warning: A business world charged with the freedoms and necessities of creativity is not a haven of peace and serenity. Remember the adage of Richard Saul Wurman: "Life is what you do next." Such a life promises excitement, opportunity, adventure, novelty, continuous meaning, and (one hopes) the forgiveness that comes with second (and third, and fourth, maybe even limitless) chances. But there is no rest in such a life: no let-up in its demands. There are no permanent kudos, either: only an occasional round of applause. On the contrary, Wurman's description of life reminds me of the old story they tell to every newsroom novice: "See that guy over there?" says the cub's self-appointed mentor, pointing to the old editor in the middle of the open room. "He's your boss, and every day you're going to go up to him and hand in your story. And every day, no matter how good that story may be, no matter if it's got Pulitzer Prize written all over it, that man will say just one thing to you, 'Okay, what are you going to do for me next?'"

"Next, please!" That's what life is always saying in a creativity-driven market. That's the wordless imperative in a jam session as well. The faint-hearted, the security-minded, the easily contented, the slacker need not apply. Everyone else will do so with high spirits and nimble imaginations. Businesses, however, have no choice in the matter. They adopt a cultural and organizational framework of "Next, please!" or, quite simply, they go out of business. Jam or die—the issue is that stark.

RIFFS

▶ It's essential that we keep the old "hard" imagery of the factory along with the "soft" imagery of music.

▶ In the future, all will live, work, and succeed, according to the principle of interdependency: ideas dependent on successful products, successful products dependent on ideas, and both dependent on the effective management of creativity.

▶ It's not enough to be creative if you cannot execute. It's not enough to execute if what you make is something that people don't want. It's not enough to execute and be creative if you don't have the structures and culture to be viable long-term.

▶ Mastery involves being able to go, not just from zero to one, to the creative result, but from one to zero, back to the beginner's mind.

▶ The creative process is an exploration that is never finished—a journey that never ends.

▶ The temporary is the rule: Creative destruction is the order of the day.

Epilogue

THE CREATIVITY TOOLKIT
A Guidebook for Monday Morning

Here's a toolkit to address the proverbial Monday morning questions about creativity. I can easily imagine a dedicated businessperson saying, "This is all well and good, this creativity stuff, as far as it goes. I read *Jamming*. But how is it going to help me on Monday morning? How is it going to change the way I run my business? What should I do first? What is my implementation plan?" Ladies and gentlemen, we've come to the bottom line.

All of us have our own versions of the Monday morning question. We all know that brilliant weekend inspiration must stand up to the harsh scrutiny of weekday judgment. Creativity, as we've repeatedly said, is about both the inspiration of art and the rigors of discipline, about weekends and Monday mornings. Like jazz, it's fueled by passion and intuition, and it is sustained through discipline. Jazz musicians don't just play whatever they feel like. Creativity must also be supported, guided, and enabled by a form, a practice, a method—in other words, by concrete realities that require structure and attention to detail. It is nothing without action.

This chapter presents a step-by-step guide to the discipline of creativity. We will look at the Monday morning questions from the perspectives of individuals, managers, and leaders.

INDIVIDUALS

Define the creative problem. For an individual, this is where creative work begins. The challenge is to shape your creative inspiration, to transform your insights into ideas you can work with. This becomes the framework within which the creative process unfolds.

Clear the mind. Creativity comes to a mind that is receptive. You want a blank sheet of mental paper. A mind full of pre-existing thoughts will have little room for new ones. This doesn't require going to a Zen monastery. A few minutes in a dark, quiet room are all it takes for some people. Others find their mind is cleared by a brisk walk, some laps in a pool, a short time listening to music. Whatever technique you choose, the more you use it, the more effective it becomes.

Activate the imagination. The imagination is like a muscle: it strengthens through use. And nothing uses it better than looking into the future, say 25 years from now, as a way of forcing your thinking beyond the domain of what you know. Design a 2020 Ford Taurus. Draw the Manhattan skyline in 2030. Envision a new breed of horses. Ignoring all limits of resources, science, and logic, invent five category-busting products. Force your thinking into the unknown to trigger insights and unleash ideas.

Wish. Choosing the right language can trigger dreams. When you say "I wish," you focus attention on what you desire, value, or hope is possible, not what is necessarily feasible or practical. Choosing the right language can activate possibilities. Wishes mobilize your passion. They will not (and should not) all be acted on, but they are vitally important in unleashing potential.

Get a fresh perspective. What would someone from a motorcycle gang have to say about your idea? How would a 12-year-old child respond? Go down the street and ask the guy behind the deli counter.

Shake up your routine. Change your workspace, your work habits, your route to work, your schedule, whom you talk to, whom you don't talk to—anything to rattle your familiar frame of reference, to jolt your mind from its usual habits. Read only business books? Buy a novel. Into *Consumer Reports*? Read *Soldier of Fortune*.

Find your woodshed. Just as the artist has his or her studio, you need a woodshed, a place that stimulates your creative processes, that is free of obligations. Some people prefer a silent room far from the fray; others like to be in the thick of the human circus. Paris cafes are legendary for triggering inspiration. Hotel rooms are well-known refuges to writers in creative crunches. I'm writing these words, for example, in an Amsterdam hotel room. And my friend, Danny Hillis, finished his dissertation on massively parallel computers only by locking himself in a Disney World hotel room until the task was complete. The flow of new ideas is the most valuable—and most vulnerable—part of the creative journey. Once this flow has started, nothing must be allowed to interrupt it. Einstein said he got his best ideas while in the shower. When you find your "shower"—don't get out (being waterlogged is a small price to pay for creative gold).

Expect to be creative. Athletes who approach the starting line imagining a win are more likely to succeed than those who doubt their abilities.

Keep track of the process. Creativity is intangible work. To support it, you need to make it tangible. The Virgin Group's Richard Branson jots down inspirations in his ubiquitous blank notebooks. Just talking about your creative challenge can help to make it more real. Find someone to bear witness to your creative initiatives. Try giving each one a name.

MANAGERS

Know your role. The first step for a creativity manager is to know what your job is. It isn't about micromanaging creative processes and people. It isn't about command and control. It's about establishing boundaries and defining the problem. In jamming terms, this means picking the tune, its key, and its tempo, then setting the agenda—when to start and when to end. Next, there's the arrangement—figuring out what combination of instruments will produce the best sound— and being extremely selective about who gets to play. The manager also helps to create an identity for the team. Great music groups have names, logos, and identifying trademarks. So should great teams.

Be protective. Your team is your baby. Guard it fiercely. Premature or abrasive judgment is a threat to your baby's health. Passionately defend free, open, even off-the-wall interaction. Make it safe. A colleague at Harvard Business School—where MBA candidates present ideas in front of as many as a hundred peers—puts it this way: "Our business here is to make our students brave."

Use theatrical gestures. A startling or vivid gesture can clear and turbocharge the group mind, whether it be a new location, activity or expectation, metaphor or combination of people. Send your team off to a cabin in the woods. Or to Formula 1 Racing School.

Secure a creativity "hot zone." Your team needs a physical environment that's both safe and stimulating. It should also reflect their preferences in terms of formality, i.e. rehearsal space vs. concert hall. Ask team members which they prefer—a small room or an airy loft? A plush sofa or a straight-back chair? A plate of sandwiches or a tofu lasagna? The latest computer technology or just paper and pencils? Your goal is to create a space where your team can soar. There are no rules, only results. Don't try to impose. Instead, listen and respond.

Create microcultures. You want your team to have a strong sense of identity and unity. Logos and trademarks help, as does a vivid metaphor for the team's challenge. Language, symbolic acts, well-timed events, and the creation of relevant expectations are all microcultural elements. Help your team through events that support bonding; recognize their successes; support them when they come up empty-handed.

Master the art of conversation. Conversation—personal communication—is one of a manager's most important tools. It puts everything on the human level, precisely where creativity lives. In a sense, management occurs *through* conversation. Conversation is the way to set boundaries, assign tasks, monitor progress, state expectations, ask good questions, and provide input. A tremendous amount of creativity can be unleashed through artful conversation. Master the art of speaking positively: Nothing shuts down creativity faster than a negative or judgmental tone. Even if you hate an idea, respect it and the person who presented it. Find ways to present criticism or feedback in an inspiring way. Finally, master the language of creativity specific to the work your team is doing.

Make time an ally. Synchronize schedules, timetables, and deadlines, even among creative folks who may view time—and resent the ticking clock—very differently from the rest of your organization.

Set boundaries. Extraordinary people often need extraordinary limits. Don't be afraid to be firm. Although creative teams may balk and squawk, they need to know there are limits to freedom.

Map creative capabilities. Pinpoint the woodsheds and hot spots. How does this map compare with the organizational chart, job descriptions, and other formal elements? Use this information as a guide to creating new hot spots. Get input from the experts.

Create places where creativity thrives. You need to provide enclaves that are appropriately insulated from the day-to-day. Too little insulation, and people will be inhibited, distracted, and ineffective. Too much, and creative work may spin freely (and expensively) out of control. Place is a key source of competitive advantage: The right enclave has the charged atmosphere that revs up talent. Relevant questions include:

▶ What is the design philosophy behind your creative enclaves? What leading-edge design principles can you incorporate?

▶ Are your enclaves appealing to creative people now in the company and to those you hope to attract?

▶ How do you know this?

▶ To what extent are the enclaves reflective of your values, and of creativity's priority in your company?

Generate a "hot set"—and then protect it. It takes time and luck to create a place where things are really happening. Once you have found it, set boundaries, limit access, encourage a sense of subculture. Keep the energy contained so that combustion can occur.

Insulate creative activity. Define protected areas for creative work. Even though it designed an office without walls, Oticon maintains private spaces that people can use when they need to be alone.

Practice the art of sitting out. Seek creativity outside the corporate walls. Korean conglomerate Samsung sends people to Palo Alto, California, to work with design firm IDEO. They set up an office and get to work learning about creativity. This provides a shelter within which new and controversial ideas can be considered outside their corporate mainstream.

Trumpet your creativity. Creativity is a powerful competitive edge, and you should let your marketplace, your organization, and the world know you've got it.

Be concrete. Make messages around creativity highly specific, descriptive, and detailed. If they can't be understood, no one will be able to act on them.

Work from the bottom up. More connection between corporate levels is essential in a creative company. The hierarchy needs to evolve into a network, the organization into a bandstand. Universally accessible online systems or voicemail can provide ways of communicating that ignore conventional hierarchies. But there are low-tech solutions as well, variations on the traditional suggestion box. In its earlier days, Lotus Development Corporation had an informal system called "The Grapevine." Collection boxes were strategically placed around the company, and anyone could write a "grape" to anyone else about any subject. Managers would measure responses to new initiatives by the number of "grapes" they received. This was an acknowledgment of the importance of the informal culture in building a climate for creativity, of the importance of bridging the formal and the informal organization.

LEADERS

Conduct a creativity audit. The Monday morning question weighs most heavily on the leaders of the organization. One friend, a CEO, put it this way: "In our business, we have to deal with a year of Mondays." Conducting a creativity audit is the first step: It clarifies the nature and extent of your creative capabilities. Creativity needs to be examined as a system, not as isolated initiatives. The goal is to understand how all the variables fit together. Done properly, the audit can lead to a complete revolution in how creativity is conceived and a plan of action implementing it. It should be a collaborative effort, for part of the audit's job is to raise awareness. The following list of questions should get you started. Get out your pencil.

► How good are we at managing creativity? Rate yourself on a spectrum of the best . . . the worst.

► When was the last time your company hit a creative home run?

► What makes you think you can do it again?

► What hard-to-copy capabilities do you have in place that allow your company to create continuously and effectively? What capabilities do you need?

► When was the last time you got really excited about an idea? What was that idea?

► When was the last time you had an in-depth discussion about your company's strategy for creativity?

▶ Do these conversations happen on a regular, or at least irregularly regular, basis?

▶ What concrete steps are you taking to be the most creative company in your industry, both today and in the future?

Just as financial audits have hard, objective measurements, so too does the creativity audit. Every company is an idea factory: its people, capital, and infrastructure combine to yield a continuous flow of ideas. The metaphor of the idea factory helps us think about how to structure and systematize creative processes. Creativity is not a "product" in a conventional sense, and the idea factory is not necessarily a tangible place. And yet every company's creativity is measurable using a number of objective criteria, including:

▶ The asset value of your idea factory—your capabilities for generating creativity.

▶ The productivity of your idea factory—for example, the number of ideas it generates, the number that have been turned into products, the percent of revenue gained from ideas less than five years old.

▶ The inventory in your idea bank, the work in progress flowing through your creative pipelines.

▶ The investment you are willing to make in your creative ideas and capabilities: What are you willing to spend in the creation of new knowledge, in information technology that supports creative collaboration?

▶ The systems you have in place to measure creative performance.

▶ The latest inventory of your knowledge assets and the capabilities you have for generating more. For example, what skills do your people have? Are they the right skills? What are you doing to help to develop new ones?

▶ The metrics you use and the way they translate into a management approach.

Establish a review process. Decide how frequently you want to audit your creativity and who will be responsible for doing it, who the audience for the findings will be, and how you plan to translate the findings into action. Establish consensus about what the relevant issues are. Get help from the outside if you need it.

Design your system. If your review has turned up serious shortfalls, you need to design a system that will foment creativity in your organization. Study what other companies have done. Again, get outside help if you need it. Ask for a wide range of input and then design a system that is right for you.

Track variables. Yves Dubriel of Renault tracks the quantity of ideas generated by his teams as a proxy for the performance of those teams. What are your tracking methods?

Benchmark. Benchmarking creative performance is crucial. The race is won not with creativity as an absolute or in a vacuum, but with what might be called *relevant creativity*—how you're doing relative to competitors' performance. Do you know the answers to the following questions? If not, why not?

▶ How much do you know about your competitors' creative capabilities?

▶ How are you doing relative to your competition in the time it takes you to develop ideas into finished product, in the quality of your creative environment, and in the attrition rate of key creators?

Keep your eyes and ears open. Establish a scanning capability that keeps you informed of what your competitors are doing vis-a-vis creativity.

Network. Talk to customers, suppliers, industry experts, business journalists, in an effort to gain diverse perceptions of your company and industry. Go to trade shows. Read, comment on, and contribute to industry publications. Keep your Rolodex up to date.

Increase awareness. Without awareness, the organization is flying blind. You need the big picture to thrive. That means allowing new input to penetrate a company's boundaries, to challenge its institutional defenses and prejudices. Lack of this awareness leads to the worst kind of myopia: that of an organization lumbering into the future unable to see the pitfalls ahead. Awareness must be systematically cultivated. It often comes from the conceptual and cognitive divergence created when the right mix of people and resources are thrown together. Management must understand the principles of good corporate cooking. Here are some questions you can ask:

▶ What specific mechanisms of awareness does your company have in place to bring in the raw materials that lead to new ideas? Who is responsible? To what extent is awareness managed as a corporate function?

▶ To what extent do your people have the process skills needed to foster new ideas instead of rehashing old ones, or to place the inherent merit of a given idea over political expediency?

▶ How does your organization cultivate the beginner's mind that can lead to originality, not a rehash of what is already known?

See for yourself. Leaders must come down from the ivory tower to practice the *Prince and the Pauper* principle: going incognito on an expedition to see how things really work.

Buy awareness. Hire a company—for example, the Institute for the Future or the Global Business Network—that peers over the horizon and comes back with fresh ideas about your competitive environment.

Live with the customer. In the age of online networks, processes can be flexibly reframed to deliver unprecedented customer intimacy. Procter & Gamble lives with Wal-Mart through its EDI strategy. VeriFone puts its people directly into the customer's environment. The gains, not only of customization and speed, but also of the quality and quantity of learning, are significant.

Increase the quantity of information. When Lou Gerstner took over IBM, he ordered 50,000 subscriptions to *Wired* magazine—to get his executives in tune with the new information technology culture.

Get fresh viewpoints. Input from divergent perspectives shouldn't come just from a board of directors, but also from advisers and a range of "friends of the company."

Map processes. Mapping a process can lead to a greater understanding of where creativity really happens, what stimulates it, and how it evolves. Mapping is useful because perceptions often differ on how things work in an organization. A leader may get the official perspective when, in fact, a company's informal culture knows where the logjams really occur. This is analogous to trying to find the hottest jazz club in a new city. You don't go to the tourist bureau. Instead, you track down musicians or owners of hot jazz clubs in other cities. Relevant mapping questions include:

► How does your idea factory work? What is its structure? What slows it down? Speeds it up?

► Where do ideas start? Who gets to define a creative problem? How do ideas progress from brainstorms to formally recognized and funded projects? In Hollywood parlance: Who gets to turn the red light to yellow to "blinking green" and finally to green? Who

are the gatekeepers? Are they appropriate or dysfunc-
tional, bureaucratic or judgmental?

▶ How much of the process is "out of the box," involving
collaboration, especially among people who are not
connected in the formal organizational chart, who
have radically·different functions, specialties, skills, or
points of view?

*Make a map of your organization in terms of its creative capa-
bilities*. Where are the woodsheds? The jazz clubs? Where are
new ideas generated? How does this map compare with the
organizational chart, job descriptions, and other formal elements? Where are the "real" hot spots preferred by the
cognoscenti, creators in the know? Make mapping a collaborative process.

*Make a map of your organization in terms of the virtual
"spaces"* in which creative work and collaboration take place.
This includes, but is by no means limited to computer networks, groupware, knowledge representation systems, online systems, videoconferencing technology, etc. How much
of your creativity place could become a creativity "space?"

Consider spinning out your creative child. This means giving
part of your company geographical autonomy. You want it to
feel like an upstart, to recreate the "leaky roof" culture that
existed in the salad days. For example, Iris, the company lead
by Ray Ozzie that developed Lotus Notes, was a spin-out
from Lotus. Even though it was subsequently spun-in and
repurchased by Lotus, it still retains its independent status
and is geographically isolated from the rest of the company.

Create a central jamming room. The consulting firm Cap Gemini commissioned Art Technology Group, a Boston-based design company, to create a technology-laden room that facilitates project management, collaboration, and the creation of new knowledge.

Tear down the walls of formal organization. What better way to both symbolize and enable the free flow of creative ideas? Oticon is the model here.

Instill belief. Creativity must be supported by belief at all levels of the organization. Leaders must make creativity an imperative of the organization's culture. Relevant questions include tests of a robust culture of creativity:

► Links creativity to strategy and managerial systems.

► Supports positive attitudes to ideas and idea generation while striking a balance with business imperatives.

► Defines specific goals and aspirations, then communicate them throughout the organization along with the belief in their achievability.

► Is highly specific with regard to desired behavior. In a sense, a successful culture embodies an approach to human nature. It is not about defining a general set of PR department platitudes along the lines of "we value creativity and strive to foster it in every area of our company."

▶ Is motivating and understandable. Can be personalized and is not overly abstract. Can generate a useful level of buy-in at all levels of the organization.

▶ Is effectively deployed (marketed) within the organization. The company does a good job of teaching its culture to its people.

▶ Provides flexible guidelines for behavior, is not a straitjacket. Does not unduly limit consideration of new ideas.

▶ To what extent does your culture explicitly address the need for creativity?

▶ Does your behavior reflect the value that you have placed on creativity?

▶ Does your company have a language for creativity that is specific and meaningful?

▶ Is your culture supported by retention of key creative talents or contradicted by their high rate of departure?

▶ Do you have meaningful measurements of culture in your organization?

Define your corporate credo. Certain values seem fundamental to a climate for creativity. Here is one version of a core set:

▶ Experiments must be unrestrained.

▶ Noble failure is honorable.

▶ Creativity is a continuous revolution.

▶ Everyone is creative.

▶ All ideas are welcome.

▶ Premature closure and excessive judgment are cardinal sins.

▶ Creativity is about the balance of art and discipline.

Craft a creativity challenge. Like Kolind with his credo of *Think the Unthinkable*, the leader of an organization must craft a meaningful creativity challenge, which should balance freedom and discipline, unite the team members behind the creative effort, and evince empathy for the difficulties of the creative process.

Find symbolic acts and concepts that reinforce culture. Many companies make symbolic appointments. Examples include, chief knowledge officer (Monitor), corporate terrorist (EDS), chief instigator (Wired).

Create a "brand identity" for creativity. Examine the possibilities of a logo, a symbol, and opportunities for merchandising creativity. Find ways of making the value of creativity tangible.

Create metaphors and mythologies for your creative enterprise. Stories and legends of any culture crystallize a deeper level of understanding and often galvanize action. When our ancestors wished to impart the essence of their cultures, they didn't give us a procedure manual. They told stories about their heroes and gave us something to emulate. Metaphors are the currency of organizational change. The stories they can crystallize lead to a deeper level of understanding and galvanize action.

Encourage the maverick identity. In Paris in the late 1800s, many Impressionist painters couldn't get their work exhibited, so they created a *salon de refusé*—a gallery for refuseniks, if you will. What began as a rebel alliance quickly became a recognized subculture as tastes caught up with the quality of the paintings. In a contemporary example, Nicholas Negroponte describes the MIT Media Lab as a digital *salon de refusé*, a place where technology visionaries, with no obvious place in the academic establishment, band together to create the new and the extraordinary.

Link creativity to strategy. Make the creative culture an integral part of the big picture. Stress creativity at the highest levels and innermost circles of governance.

People. If I ran a large company, it is the human agenda that would make me stay up late at night worrying. Without the right talent, you've got nothing. The idea factory doesn't work without the individual "brain factories" to make it happen. Thus it is that the leader of the organization must be a casting agent. People *are* your capabilities, today and tomorrow. I would want to know the answer to such questions as the following:

▶ Who are the top creative talents in your company? Name three.

▶ Who are the top creative talents in your industry and how do your people compare with them?

▶ What do you have in place that ensures their loyalty to you?

▶ How many key creative talents did you lose in the past twelve months and what have you done to replace them?

▶ What are you doing to develop new creative talent?

▶ Do you have the right people for creative results? What makes you so sure? How do you know that the people you don't have or wouldn't hire aren't exactly the kind of people you need and should have?

▶ Do you reward your creative people appropriately? What is the theory of compensation underlying your approach to rewarding creative people? What to do?

Be fussy about who you hire. The intimacy of creative work requires the right people. This doesn't necessarily mean people who are easy to get along with, but rather people who add to the creative mix, who bring with them divergent perspectives and skills that create the possibility of creative abrasion. Creative organizations have very particular environments. You'll save a lot of time (and mistakes) by being choosy.

Invent your own diagnostic screens. For example, First Virtual Corporation simply shows people their bull-pen working environment. If people don't like it or look nervous, they're not hired. The point is to develop a custom diagnostic that determines fit between a potential new hire and the organization.

Track flows of talent in and out of the company, especially if you're very large.

Reward by cash and noncash compensation. Compensation is a way of sculpting behavior. It is true that creators don't create for money alone, yet creativity is not about pure philanthropy either. Consider novel methods, for example, pooling compensation. Screenwriters, once at the bottom of the Hollywood totem pole, are getting a new deal from DreamWorks SKG. There, in contrast with industry custom, net profits are defined meaningfully; writers will enjoy an actual-back end payoff from their creative labors. In breaking with current custom, DreamWorks is adopting a retro model in which writers will have a longer-term relationship with DreamWorks extending beyond the transactions surrounding a specific project. If films begin with "the word," then creativity at DreamWorks will begin with a feeling of community on the part of a group of carefully selected writers, who will inhabit a '90's version of the traditional "writer's wing." To reinforce this sense of community, a portion of their compensation will be pooled. Each writer will share in the upside of all the projects generated by the DreamWorks writing community; hence the motivation to share ideas and provide encouragement "for the greater good."

Beware of the demotivating aspects of financial competition, but don't hesitate to top the competition's offer if you need a creative talent for the strategic advancement of your enterprise. Some industries, especially new ones, contain a very limited number of key creators. The video game industry in the early 1980s was described as having fewer than 100 top designers. It was described by one industry expert as a situation in which, "If you don't have the horses, you can't run."

Intentionally hire people who don't fit the mold. Bring in outsiders, young people, people who break the mold entirely by virtue of their style, expertise, or perspective. In the words of Stanford professor Bob Sutton, consider hiring people who make you feel uncomfortable and who don't fit in.

Training. This is a crucially important dimension of investment. Senco not only invests in education but in employee-run symposia. It is also important to invest in skills that may not be obvious or that may have no immediate payoff.

Be Captain Kirk. Captain Kirk succeeds because he has a psychologically diverse team that he manages well: Mr. Spock (logic), Dr. McCoy (emotions), and Scotty (details). Assemble diverse teams that have the flavor of rebel alliances, skunkworks, cross-functional teams, tiger teams. Composing unlikely teams can increase creative abrasion. Xerox Parc does this consciously with its PAIRS (PARC Artists in Residence) program. Lars Kolind's notion of multi-job also increases diversity and is a way of dissolving narrow specialties. Networking within the creative community can also increase your capabilities.

Embrace new technologies. New technologies create new capabilities. Leaders need to understand the status of the corporate "nervous system"—computer networks, groupware, and other technologies capable of acquiring, interpreting, and distributing knowledge. This nervous system is a proxy for institutional memory, and it enhances creative possibility by providing a virtual "space" for it and allowing different points of view to catch on. Relevant questions include:

► What enabling technologies do you have in place? Inventory your use of such modalities as voicemail, e-mail, groupware, and knowledge management systems.

► To what extent does technology increase interaction among your people? How literate are your people in these new technologies?

► Do you understand how to manage collaboration in the "wired" organization?

► If you're not wired, is your MIS department capable of doing the job?

► How alert are you to the availability of new technologies?

Maintain awareness of new technologies as they become available. The pace of change is only accelerating. While the time to start is definitely whenever you're ready, the time until the next upgrade is probably a lot sooner than you think.

Experiment with novel technologies including computer assisted brainstorming, and using audiovisual media to represent knowledge and to describe organizational processes.

Experiment with creating new process flows. These experiments can be carried incrementally, with a single team to start with, as opposed to an entire organization. Pilot implementation outside the boundaries of the existing MIS department can be a low-cost investment, a few software licenses, and some facilitation.

IF YOU ARE VERY LARGE

If you are very large, there are both challenges and opportunities. Size can be an asset. For example, a large organization is typically multicultural either because of diversity within one national environment, or because the company is multinational. Being *multicultural* leads to an ongoing opportunity for knowledge arbitrage. It can be a benefit to have "many accents" as Sergio Zyman at Coca-Cola is fond of saying.

Second, it is important to integrate *creativity as an agenda item in strategic planning* and the monitoring of performance. The tasks of leadership around creativity become even more complex as the "congregation" becomes larger. This leads to further need for systems that will support creativity, i.e., the idea factory on an even larger scale.

Reviewing creative capabilities is important, not just on a particular occasion, but on an on-going basis. It should be a process not an event. Is an appropriate metric for you about tracking excitement and fun? Is it tracking the volume of idea generation as is the case with Renault? Is it tracking the flow of talent in and out of the organization? *Finding the right metrics and using them* are crucially important in the very large organization where leaders must "fly-by-wire" and lack the moment-to-moment, hands-on feeling of flying the plane.

The relevant systems may include capabilities for *institutionalizing awareness*, especially as it concerns benchmarking relative to competition. This may lead to a number of *make versus buy decisions*, hiring, for example, organizations whose specialty is scanning the environment for relevant input as well as keeping pace with enabling technology.

Information technology becomes even more important as an integrating influence and as a way of establishing flexible boundaries around creative projects, of imposing a needed degree of informality, and intimacy for creativity on the large structured organization. It is also crucially important as a mechanism for allowing the organization to manage knowledge, to perceive its environment, to represent knowledge, to deploy that knowledge internally, to learn and to advance, to use Senco's language. Finally, a company's leaders must be alert to new technologies, a job in many cases too important to be left to conventional MIS stakeholders.

Regarding organizational structure, very large companies can capitalize on adopting some variation of the *studio model*. They can use their brand, access to information, scale, capital, and access to distribution as magnets to attract independent production talent. This can set the rules of competition in which the key success factors become finding talent, packaging talent with opportunities and resources, branding initiatives, and maintaining continuous awareness of the environment.

Large organizations can also act as *service stations for independent contractors*. They can use their resources to create an infrastructure that attaches talent to themselves without having to, or aspiring to "own" that talent.

Another novel way of organizing becomes capitalizing on *alumni networks*. The old contract of employer-employee gives way to more encompassing relationships we have seen in the cases of Bain & Company and First Virtual Corporation. The astute organization must understand that people who leave the organization do not necessarily stop their ability to add value, whether it is in terms of awareness of the environment, sourcing opportunities, or carrying out work on a part-time or sitting in basis. Figuring out what the glue is to attract these people as Bain has done by making available portions of its information infrastructure and toolset to talented professional alumni, poses an important set of opportunities for the large organization in search of the right relationship with talent.

Because of their very size, *managing the institutional belief system* is what brings it all together. Collective beliefs are like the rudder that guides the overall direction of the ship and connects individual aspirations to corporate goals. In the large organization, communicating belief is crucially important to ensure the continuing relevance of the culture. This relates to Jan Carlzon's adage that all business is show business. The person at the top must be like a media mogul who is able to use every tool at his or her disposal to communicate the culture with relevance. The leader's job is also to institutionalize tolerance and even appetite for constant change, to buffer the insults of change and to make them worth pursuing. It is also to make sure that the culture is continually relevant to the challenges ahead.

Regarding place, the leader must make a host of make vs. buy decisions, sitting in vs. sitting out, and the establishment of enclaves that at the same time avoid the sterility of large, bureaucratic laboratories. Awareness may be a function that must be outsourced. For many reasons, the very large organization faces the imperative of developing special skills at managing alliances in a way that accrues to the benefit of the organization.

LEADERSHIP AND CHANGE

At the organizational level, the issues of managing creativity are analogous to those of running a record label. The job is no longer hands-on management of creative people or working with and through a particular musical group; it is creating an environment in which many creators can do their work. It involves attending to higher order questions such as the "sound" of the record label, defining standards of quality, and picking people who pick the people and do the actual creative work. The tone of the organization comes from its leaders, as do surprise, delight and fun for the people in it. If it doesn't exist in its leaders, chances are it won't exist in the organization either. As a performing art, leadership is just as creative as the underlying creative work itself. It is no less about creativity than designing the new culture, the new paradigm, the new deal, the new system.

Being the agent and champion of change—Change begins at the top as a creative task in and of itself. Astute leaders follow the rules of creative process themselves in finding their own woodshed for recreating their organizations.

Leading change is itself about creativity—The leader may need some isolation in order to clear away the mind, space, and beliefs of his or her organization. For example, Kolind drafted Think the Unthinkable on retreat in order to redesign the culture and organization of Oticon as his own blank canvas for creative expression. Ralph Ungermann was in transition from a previous company to a new startup when he developed the organizational plan for First Virtual Corporation. Jan Carlzon turned to an off-shore resource, an advertising agency, as a creative "lab" in which to begin reframing the new culture of Scandinavian Airlines System. Investor Richard Rainwater and MIT Media Lab director Nicholas Negroponte share at least one attribute in common. Neither has a permanent office. Their nomadic lifestyles allow them a constant state of beginner's mind. They become expeditionary forces of one.

Engage in the gentle art of reperceiving—This is a term coined by Pierre Wack, pioneer of scenario planning. The traditional view is to regard creativity as a happy accident, no more manageable than running around with a bottle trying to capture lightning. What we have proposed is a way of managing creativity in an intentional and systematic fashion. What is required urgently is first to see creativity as a complete end-to-end process. The stakes are high. The goal must be nothing less than creating the leadership position in your company's industry, investing in hard-to-copy capabilities, finding ways to intellectually dominate your opportunity set so as to redefine the competition and in so doing to realize competitively meaningful growth through creativity.

Craft a meaningful challenge—Like Kolind with his credo of *Think the Unthinkable*, the leader of an organization must craft a meaningful challenge for it. Criteria for an effective challenge as we have said in chapter 7 include the extent to which it uses language effectively, acknowledges a stimulating context, links the "mouth" and the "money," is appropriately prepared, involves an appropriate level of discipline, leads to a feeling of complicity, and evinces empathy for the difficulties of the creative process.

Making creativity an organizational priority—Throughout the process of change, a company's leaders must engender a feeling of belief in creativity by presenting it to the organization as a priority. Remember Douglas Ivester's words about creativity, "We believe in it—we're going to insist on it." The leader is responsible for admitting the discussion of creativity to the highest levels and innermost circles of corporate governance and discussion. The leader must be a champion of creativity, a change agent, and an architect of that change. He or she must create the environment for creativity, then champion, advocate and defend it.

Reframe the organizational belief system—This is a highly creative exercise of the skills of design. Problems must be framed in order to find optimal solutions. Choice of craft is material to the outcome. Is it marketing communications that will convey an important set of new messages both inside and outside the company? Is it the craft of culture prototyping, using devices such as Jan Carlzon's Little Red Books? Or of organizational prototyping through the flexibility to reframe collaboration that comes from groupware and the use of computer networks? Is it the dramatic craft of the leader him or herself as the evangelist for desired change, one who focuses people's attention on a new and inspiring set of challenges? What are the metaphors, icons and symbols, even props that will be relevant in this process?

Challenges must have resonance—Crafting a resonant challenge involves understanding the motivation for change and the history of creativity initiatives. Why creativity? Why now? Only by considering these questions completely can the leader craft a salient challenge.

Maintaining a state of beginner's mind. The organization's leader must be alert for signs of arrogance. It is not simply enough to go from zero to one. Part of turning creativity into an ongoing process is about *going from one back to zero*, from success back to the beginning, from expertise back to an organizational mind that is cleared. Thus, leaders need to be alert for the pathologies of success and arrogance, and continually back to fundamental questions. He or she may have to be alert for opportunities to bring in outside input, talent that "sits in," in order to refresh the internal perspective of the organization, to bring in divergent inputs, and to stimulate the creative process by bringing in different points of view. Leaders must be alert to posing questions and challenges that shock the organization into a new awareness of what is possible. They must constantly reinvent and recraft the challenge, looking at it as an asymptote, a destination that is never reached, as a continual revolution.

Orchestrate the process. Change is the sum of a thousand acts of re-perception and behavior change at every level of the organization. The leader must conduct this process as if he or she were Duke Ellington leading a large jazz orchestra. Communications must be effective, opportunities for drama must be capitalized on, limits and expectations must be set. Leaders must be empathetic to the difficulty of change. Those discomforts that can be remedied should be, while the inevitable and unavoidable discomforts of change must be endured and their lessons absorbed. This is not a process about making nice and carries certain inherent conflicts. Not everyone can get what they want. Not everyone will know what they are "supposed" to do. Not everyone will have equal appetite for the ambiguities and confusions that may result. Not everyone wants to give up power associated with the status quo. The leader's trick is to maintain the organizational sweet spot, the point of balance between change and discomfort so that what otherwise might be creative abrasion does not degenerate into mere abrasion. Growth in organizations involves accepting a certain amount of chaos, frustration, and discomfort. When properly framed, they are endurable. And the rewards can be great.

Build consensus for change. Lars Kolind orchestrated the change process at Oticon as a series of conversations that took place at company meetings. He empowered those who were the "real" doers in the company to drive the change process. These were the people who had consistently taken responsibility for making things happen that affected the welfare of the organization as a whole. He also created buy-in by involving people with the *Indretningsgruppen* or interior decoration committee, that later spawned a host of other committees ultimately involving the majority of the company's people. He practiced the art of stage management by linking Oticon's change process to larger issues of the day, for example by getting government support and media attention for Oticon as a "twenty-first century organization."

He made sure there was recognition of the importance of creativity and creative performance at all levels. He reemphasized the role of hierarchy as a factor in approving creative ideas, in linking resources to ideas, and enabling people to collaborate around new ideas. And while he allowed free discussion, he also set boundaries for the change process and for what was expected.

Traditionally, creativity has been viewed as a happy accident, no more manageable than running around with a bottle trying to capture lightning. In this book I have proposed a way of managing creativity in an intentional and systematic fashion. Twenty years ago, if you'd asked a corporate leader what his or her strategic planning process was, the response might well have been "Huh?" Today, if you ask a corporate leader what his or her system for creativity is, the response might very well be the same "Huh?" I expect that attitude is rapidly changing. The stakes are high: success or failure in the creativity-driven twenty-first century.

Jamming—The Art and Discipline of Business Creativity
is part of a larger effort to develop tools for
business practitioners that will make creativity actionable,
systematic, and continuous. Work is underway to
transform the Jamming concepts into documentary film and
video, computer software, creativity audit procedures,
and executive continuing education. For further
information, visit the Jamming website on the Internet
at http://www.jamming.com.

INDEX